Mikita Brottman takes terrifying risks but never puts a foot wrong. These stories begin with delicate precision and build stunning pace and power. This is fiction that is truer and more penetrating than the savage facts at its core.

–Katherine Dunn, author of *Geek Love*

Brottman's grimly pragmatic literary stance recalls such earlier artists of the quotidian macabre as Shirley Jackson and Flannery O'Connor: *Thirteen Girls* is an impressive successor to their stories of American dread.

–John Pistelli, *Rain Taxi*

Thirteen Girls manages the improbable feat of conjuring up the full horror and emotional devastation of serial homicide by focusing exclusively on the aftermath of the crimes and those left to deal with the consequences: family members, police officers, witnesses, survivors. Known for her brilliant, provocative cultural criticism, Mikita Brottman has produced a stunning work of crime fiction—a genuine tour de force.

–Harold Schechter, author of *The Serial Killer Files*

Also by Mikita Brottman

The Great Grisby

Hyena

House of Quiet Madness

Phantoms of the Clinic

The Solitary Vice: Against Reading

High Theory, Low Culture

Offensive Films

*Funny Peculiar: Gershon Legman and the
Psychopathology of Humor*

Car Crash Culture

Meat is Murder!

Hollywood Hex

Thirteen Girls

MIKITA BROTTMAN

NINE-BANDED
BOOKS

Second printing

5 4 3 2

Cover design by Kevin I. Slaughter

Editorial assistance: Ann Sterzinger

Thirteen Girls ©2012, 2014 Mikita Brottman

ISBN 10: 0990733505
ISBN 13: 978-0-9907335-0-8

Nine-Banded Books
P.O. Box 1862
Charleston, WV 25327
NineBandedBooks.com

...the crack in the tea-cup opens
A lane to the land of the dead.

—W.H. Auden

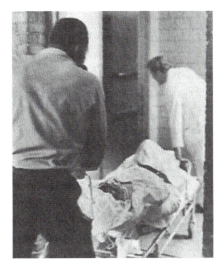

1. Lisa

I lie in bed at night, and wonder: Did Lisa call for me as she lay there across the front seat of Joey's car, her beautiful blonde hair turning red from her own lost blood? When those thoughts come, I try to remind myself: Whoever would have been there that night in that particular spot would have been killed. It could have been anybody. He did not choose Lisa on purpose. He was not looking on purpose for the most perfect girl.

The kennel where I work is full of abandoned dogs, all haunted by terrible unknown pasts, some with their ears cut by scissors. Now, by no fault of their own, they're waiting to be "put down" (murdered). I try to place them with families. I have placed over one hundred dogs this year alone, including: Boxers, Terriers, Chihuahuas, Dachshunds, Pekes, and Border Collies. Those who don't find homes, when their time is up they are gassed. There was a momma Maltese and eight tiny puppies that were supposed to be put down yesterday morning, but a sanctuary in Jersey was able to take them at the last minute. I took in a Pit Bull myself for a while. Her puppies are probably due any day now. She's safe in rescue, taken care of.

When Lisa got home from work, she'd change into her cutoff jeans and sit with me in the kitchen while I peeled potatoes at the sink. She'd had a long, hard day in the city. I didn't expect her to help me with dinner, but she always did. Coco, her little Yorkie mix, would sit at her feet and beg while Lisa sang to her, feeding her crusts of bread and biscuit crumbs. Coco is here with me right now as I write. These days, my heart is with the animals.

The animals. There are so many tragedies, especially in the holiday season. A couple days before Christmas we get people dumping their adult dogs because, oh, we're getting a new puppy and we don't want this old one anymore. So what are they going to do when the new puppy gets old? There was a chocolate Lab at the kennel today, such a fun dog. Can you believe someone gave him up? I just could not believe it. Somebody just threw him out. Unbelievable. He was such a good boy. And then as soon as Christmas is over, we get the breeders who didn't sell all their stock coming into the animal shelter saying oh, I mysteriously found these three and four week old puppies, and their mother was nowhere to be found, so here, take them. I'm like, Ma'am, I'm sorry, but I know you've been breeding these little fellas and trying to sell them in the classified ads for three weeks because don't think I'm not looking. We report them to animal control and they get charged with abandonment.

Weekend mornings Lisa would wake up slowly, sleeping in late, groggy from the night before. I'd wait till eleven then go to her.

Come on, Mom, let me sleep, she'd say. I was up till one-thirty last night.

One-thirty? Are you sure you don't mean three-thirty? That girl!

She was never home before three on the weekends.

When she finally got out of bed, she'd slip silently into the kitchen. Even if my back was turned, I knew she was there. Her presence was so strong. She'd always brighten my mornings with her beautiful smile, always singing, laughing, making fun of me.

Hey, Mom, she'd tease. Where are my chocolate pancakes? Don't you remember? Last night you promised me chocolate pancakes!

Well, I never promised, but of course I'd make chocolate pancakes for her—how could I refuse?—and she'd soak them in maple syrup and happily devour a whole pile. Lisa had an appetite like a horse but then she was only twenty, still growing, she never seemed to put on weight. Did I mention she was beautiful? Five foot two with blonde hair and brown eyes. An angel. Everyone said so. Her natural hair was chestnut brown, but she lightened it with bleach and it came out just darling. She was trying to look older, but it was impossible, with her tiny dimples and laughing baby face filled with sunshine.

New York was a broken place back when the girls were young, but for some reason—I don't know why—it felt friendlier back then. People would hang out on the streets more, at the ice truck, outside the souvlaki stand. It felt like you knew everybody in the neighborhood. Walking down Union, you'd see guys washing their cars, people sitting on fire escapes smoking, listening to music, watching the girls walk by.

Lisa and Terri both grew up overnight, and suddenly they were wearing tight jeans and T-shirts, and Lisa had dyed her hair. All at once there were boys everywhere. Lisa and Terri would be getting ready upstairs while Daddy and I would sit in the living room with their dates. We would look at these boys, at their faces and their white vests and heeled shoes, and wonder: How could we possibly know? They could be junkies, bums, sex maniacs for all we knew. We wanted to ask them what they had in mind, whether they'd ever used dope, but of course we couldn't ask them anything like that, so we just sat there being polite, drinking Pepsi, waiting for the girls to come downstairs.

Joey was a nice-looking young man. Lisa thought he looked like Mark Spitz, the swimmer, and she was right. He had a moustache like all the boys did back then, and that night he wore a blue shirt with an open neck. Lisa wore her peasant blouse and a mid-length denim skirt. Everyone seemed to dress better back then. Girls would perm their hair. Guys would wear slick white suits over polo neck sweaters like John Travolta.

We watched them leave, looking down from the terrace. Joey even opened the car door for her when they left. Daddy said: Geez, look at that, I haven't seen a kid do that in years.

Lisa waved up at us, then she was in the car and they had gone. I didn't even kiss her goodbye. How I wish I'd held my darling child one last time, kissed her beautiful face. What is really valuable in life, you learn. These things we fret about, are they really so important? Now I know to be thankful for what I've been given.

Lisa dated a lot, and who could blame her? I, for one, did not. She was a lovely, healthy, beautiful young girl, and she worked so hard during the week. She loved to go out on Friday and Saturday nights, but the thing a lot of people don't know about her is that she was a true romantic. She wanted to be swept off her feet. She was looking for the kind of man who'd lay down his life for her. I always said it was her Daddy's fault. He spoiled them. He was devoted. No matter what, he was ready to sacrifice anything for his girls. But most of Lisa's dates were just ordinary neighborhood guys, and they always let her down. She deserved better, and she knew it.

The newspapers all called Joey Lisa's boyfriend, but he was not. She had just broken off her engagement with a fellow named Paul Giuliano. They had a fight a few days earlier. It had happened before. Paul was in love with her, and I still believed they would get married. She let Joey take her out on a date, but it was nothing serious.

Joey had spotted the girls at a club on the west side a couple of days earlier. He saw them walk in. You could hardly miss them, a blonde and a brunette. They always caused a sensation when they went out together. The boys were all over them. They were having a talent show that night, and Terri had won an audition. Terri wanted to be a singer. She still has a beautiful voice. Joey went over and started talking. It was Terri he liked at first. I'm sure he thought Lisa was out of his league. Terri was only fifteen, though, much too young for him, so he started talking to Lisa, and he was surprised how friendly she was. They hit it off. But then, Lisa hit it off with everybody.

We always thought she would go to college, but she was too full of life. Lisa was super smart, but she didn't like school, she couldn't wait to leave. She went straight into business. Her first job was operating a Telex machine, then she got her job at the fabric company, which was much more suitable, given her talents. We were very proud of her.

That night, Joey was taking her to see *Saturday Night Fever* at the Parkway Theater. The movie started at ten, and she called me from the lobby just before they went in. Lisa was a good girl.

She'd always call to let us know she was okay.

Everything's fine, Mom, she told me. Joey's a real gentleman.

After the movie was over, around midnight, they went to a club, but they didn't stay long. They drove down to the bay and stopped for coffee and a late night snack. In the coffee shop, Lisa remembered she'd promised to call Angie Martin, her best friend. She called at one-thirty in the morning, but that was normal for those girls. They never went to sleep. After hanging up, she left the coffee shop with Joey and walked back to the car. On the way, they stopped under a streetlamp to watch the full moon on the water. Like I said, Lisa was a romantic. They held hands and walked to the sea wall, looking out at the bay. They crossed the footbridge, went into the playground and rode the swings for a while.

The hardest time in the day for me is dinnertime. Every day, peeling potatoes reminds me of her. She'd always pick up a loaf of rye bread on her way back from the subway, from Mazzola's, on Henry and Union. Here now in the kitchen, empty without her, I stand at the sink peeling potatoes, and my tears fall into the bowl.

How is it that she is gone, my Lisa, such a force of life, my absolute everything? Why on this cruel earth did it have to be my Lisa, my first-born child? Where has she gone, my angel with her delicate long fingers, her lovely arms, her face shining with joy? Now all I have are photographs, her clothes, her silver jewelry box, her green necklace, her little dog.

At first I thought I would never recover. I told the doctor: All the medicine I need is my Lisa alive, here with me at the table, sharing breakfast with me. Then one morning I woke up crying, and all of a sudden my tears just dried up and I knew, in my head, they're going to catch this guy. I just knew. They were going to catch him. And they did.

Lisa had not been worried. She joked about him, in fact. She was a blonde, after all, and we lived in Queens. All the other killings had been brunettes, and in Brooklyn. Terri was dark-haired, and she was frightened. He'd been walking the streets for more than a year. We were all afraid. We were paying taxes and we deserved protection. Everybody's life was in jeopardy. They should have had lights everywhere, police on patrol all the time, in all the hidden parts of the city. Everybody was afraid of what would happen when they turned the next corner.

There was a blackout that year, and lootings. Even in Queens, it was rough. There were places you just didn't go, burned-out buildings, gunshots at night, police sirens. It's easy to forget what a dangerous place it was. In the South Bronx, there were people living on fire escapes and in the burned-out shells of cars. Landlords would pay gang members fifty or a hundred dollars to burn down their buildings. I had the sense back then that the whole city was damned. I thought nothing would ever fix it. It was just chaos. Teenage pregnancies, addiction, people out of their heads on drugs lying in the street. Those shells of empty buildings were full of junkies and homeless people. In the winter, they would freeze to death in the streets.

But Lisa wasn't afraid. She was always a brave girl, very independent. Did I mention that she and her friend Angie went to Florida with their own money? She'd never flown before. It was such a thrill to her. We met her at the airport when she came back. The door swung open and there she was, our beautiful suntanned daughter in her white shorts. She brought gifts for everyone, Jewelry for me, cigars for her Daddy. She loved it, couldn't wait to go back.

He fired through the passenger window, hitting Lisa first. Four shots. One went into Joey's eye, blinding him forever. He could hear Lisa moaning, but could not see her. He was bleeding everywhere. He leaned on the car horn. When the police arrived they covered him with a blanket and lifted him out of the car. Lisa was lying across the front seat. She was conscious but she did not know what had happened. Thank God, she did not know she had been shot.

At the hospital, they said she kept asking for me, so they let me see her, just for a moment. Thank God they did. Her right eye was swollen shut and the lid was a morbid black and blue. There was dried blood in her hair. I was with her in the operating theater.

Her wounds were too serious for Coney Island, so they rushed her to King's County in an ambulance and we followed behind. At King's County, she was stabilized while they X-rayed her brain and made plans for the operation. Daddy, Terri and I went home around six to shower and change. When we got back, they'd taken her into surgery. After an hour, an Indian doctor came and told us there were two bullets in her head. One was lodged in the top of her skull. The second one had gone through her head into the base of her neck. He said this wound was critical, and there was probably brain damage. He said the bullet had fractured her skull.

She was in surgery for eight hours straight. At one point, a nurse walked by with Lisa's bra dangling from her hand. It was almost black with dried blood.

At noon, the doctor came to see us. He said in the case of Lisa's injury, frankly, the statistics did not look good. He said they were trying to remove a part of her skull casing without damaging the brain. He said they were doing the best they could.

They brought her out of the operating theater at four-thirty the next afternoon, and that's when they let us see her again. She was unconscious, covered in tubes and hooked up to machines. She did not respond when we spoke to her. Her eyes were swollen black and blue.

They said she was stable and we could go home. I had just got to sleep when the hospital called and said the pressure had built up in her brain stem and they were going to take her back into the operating theater. After the second operation, they put her in intensive care, but the brain swelling continued. She lost all her vital functions. Her heart stopped six times. The seventh time it stopped and did not start again.

2. Tracy

I was nine years old when it happened. My parents were divorced, and I didn't get to see a lot of my Dad, so I could hardly believe it when he asked if we wanted to go to Aspen. He was going to a medical conference, and he said Tracy would take us skiing. He said it would be a good opportunity for us to get to know her.

"Why is *she* going?" said Jason.

"Because she is," said Dad.

"Then forget it."

"Well that's too bad. You're going to miss out on a great trip. If you don't want to go, fine, but let's face it, you're not going to like any girl I date."

He was right. And Tracy was better than Kelly, his last girlfriend, another nurse. When she wasn't in her uniform, she wore gym clothes and gym shoes and a ponytail. She was an alcoholic who'd leave messages for Mom in our mailbox and call up with drunken rants about the president and the FBI. She drank cheap beer, and after about thirteen beers it was Tea Time, according to Jason. All of a sudden, she'd

adopt a British accent and speak like that for the rest of the night—
bloody this and bloody that. At the time, we thought it was hilarious,
but looking back it was kind of sad. She was clearly insane. When they
fired her from the hospital, she accused Dad of stealing her jewelry
and her checkbook.

One time we were at Dad's house and we heard her shout, "Go fuck
yourself!"

"Hey. That's enough," said Dad. "What do you want me to do?"

"I want you to go fuck yourself is what I want you to do, Bill." She
said he hadn't done "a damn stinking thing" for her. She said all he ever
thought about was his job and his kids.

Tracy wasn't crazy, although she sometimes did crazy things. She'd
try to make us laugh by puffing her face out and rolling her eyes. She
could do bridge, crab, handstands and cartwheels. Last time she and
Dad went to a conference, she bought us Aeropostale shirts, a red one
for me and a blue one for Jason, which was pretty nice of her, though
we figured they were really from Dad, because he paid for them. She
also gave me a striped tote bag that she said she never used any more.

On the plane from Lansing, I saw her sniffing a little bottle, and I
asked her what it was.

"Eucalyptus oil. It's a decongestant," she said. "I'm just getting over
the flu."

"What does it do?"

"Clears your sinuses. You have to be careful to use only a little sniff
because if you take too much, it's poisonous."

"No kidding," said Dad, who was sitting on Tracy's right with a glass
of scotch.

"Yes, and you know what's weird? For koala bears, it's all they eat. A human being would probably die if they ate, like, six leaves."

"Is that right?"

"Did you know that female koala bears have two vaginas?"

"No, I didn't," said Dad, "And I didn't want to know, either."

Snowmass was about a twenty-minute drive from Aspen, and in between were Buttermilk and Aspen Highlands. We rented a car and drove down 82. Tracy was sitting in the front, with Dad. They called each other "Trey" and "Billy," which made Jason turn to me and stick his fingers down his throat. Still, the more time we spent with Tracy, the more difficult it was to hate her. Even when we were on the plane, I could already feel things changing.

Snowmass was like a cowboy town, but with high-class brand-name stores, a lot of sporting goods shops, movie theaters, restaurants and nightclubs. When we got out of the car I remember how different the air felt—fresh, thin and icy.

Our hotel room had a hot tub in the bathroom, which had its own fireplace, with a ceramic bear holding the poker and tongs for the fire. While Tracy freshened up, we went out on the balcony with Dad, and there was a female deer chewing leaves from a bush. Something startled her, and she skipped off down the bank toward the stream.

That night, we ate at the Big Country Grill. We sat at a wooden table with no tablecloth, next to a window overlooking the slopes. Dad ordered steaks but Tracy said she wasn't hungry, she just wanted soup and a salad. While we ate, she told us about some of her patients at the hospital.

"There's this one lady, Mrs. Schmitz, who's sixty-five but with a mental age of eight," said Tracy. "She wets the bed every single night. And there's this other lady, Mrs. Olson, who forgets to put in her teeth, so nobody knows what she's saying. She just moves her gums around in her mouth."

"That is so gross."

"She's no trouble. She sleeps most of the day. The problem is, we're always finding her teeth in weird places, like on the coffee table in the day room, or in the ladies' bathrooms."

"That is disgusting."

"Oh, and last week? There was this old guy with real low blood pressure. When I asked him how he was doing, he said, 'Oh, honey, I'm fine. There ain't nothing wrong with me. Matter of fact, I feel like getting in my car right now and driving home.' That was three-thirty in the afternoon. By six o'clock, he was dead."

"Feel like you've got room for some pie?" asked the waitress.

We spent all the next day on the slopes. Tracy was wearing the sweater Dad had given her for Christmas, black with a red pattern at the neck, a green wool hat with a pom-pom on top, and a puffy blue jacket.

We skied at Aspen Highlands, which has runs for beginners as well as hard-core experts. When we got tired, we stood at the side and watched the jumpers twisting and turning, doing all kinds of tricks. There was even one guy skiing backwards. A lot of people were driving snowmobiles, which were like little speedboats that zipped over the snow. One man had his baby strapped to his chest while he was skiing, which did not look like a good idea.

That night, we met Dad's friend Mark Sussman for dinner at a restaurant called the Salt Cellar. Mark was also a doctor. He'd been Tracy's boyfriend before she got together with Dad, which we found kind of weird, but Dad didn't seem to care. Tracy's stomach had been bothering her all day, and she just had a glass of milk and some beef stew. Dad ordered a bottle of wine, and let Jason and me have a small glass each, mixed with Coke. We finished dinner by eight and went back to the lobby. Mark Sussman came with us. Turns out he was staying in our hotel.

Dad sat down in front of the fire, crossed his legs and picked up a copy of the *New York Times* from the table. We had comics to read. Mark had a copy of *Confidential* that he'd just finished. Tracy asked if she could read it. She said she'd trade it for her *Pandora*, and asked Dad to go to the room and get it. Dad said he wanted to warm up by the fire, and she'd have to go get it herself. I watched her getting on the elevator. She was still wearing her boots and puffy ski jacket, and she turned and smiled at me before the doors opened and she stepped inside.

She should have been gone ten minutes or less. We kept waiting for the elevator doors to open and for Tracy to step out, but it didn't happen. After half an hour, Dad started to get antsy. He went up to the room, knocked on the door, and waited. He thought maybe she'd got sick, fainting or falling and knocking her head. He came back down to the lobby and asked the receptionist for an extra key, and we all went up there. Everything was just as it had been when we'd left for dinner. Tracy's purse wasn't there, and her *Pandora* was still on the magazine stand next to the bed. She hadn't even been back to the room.

Dad asked us if we thought she was mad at him for not getting the magazine.

"No doubt," said Jason.

"She wasn't mad," I said. "She was smiling."

"You're right," said Dad. "You know what? She probably ran into some friends from the hospital. Mark, let's you and me go check out some of the other bars, see if we can't find her. You kids stay here, in case she comes back, okay?"

He wrapped a scarf round his neck and pulled on his leather gloves. He didn't seem worried, just a little pissed.

Jason and I turned on the TV and watched a movie.

When Dad got back, he said three doctors had seen Tracy get out of the elevator and walk down the hallway toward our room. He called the Aspen Police Department and they sent a patrolman over, who filled out a missing person report, then told Dad to call him in the morning if Tracy hadn't come back. She'd be back, he said, once the bars and parties had broken up. He virtually guaranteed it.

"No," Dad told him. "It's not like that. I'm telling you, she was sick."

"Alright, sir," said the cop, taking out his radio. "We'll run a quick search, see what we can do." He broadcast Tracy's description to all the other cops out on duty that night in Snowmass and Aspen: A twenty-three-year-old woman, five feet four inches tall, brown shoulder-length hair, parted in the middle, wearing ski boots, blue jeans, and a blue puffy jacket.

Dad told the police how friendly she was.

"She's real trusting," he told them. "She'll speak to anybody."

"That's unfortunate," said the cop. "It's an opportunity for people who are willing to take advantage of it." The cop thought maybe somebody had seen something and hadn't reported it. He wanted to focus on the timeline between when we last saw Tracy and when Dad called 911. We kept telling them, there was no timeline. She just got on the elevator. That was all.

We didn't get a lot of sleep that night. Dad was up late, talking on the phone. I don't know all the people he called, but I know one of them was Tracy's mom in Lansing.

The next morning, the cops came back and asked us lots of questions about Tracy—when we'd last seen her, what she was wearing, what kind of mood she'd been in. We told them everything we knew. At one point, the cop said that since Tracy was over eighteen, it could be she just left of her own free will. Dad told them it was impossible, but I don't know if they believed him. They kept asking him if he and Tracy had a fight.

"Absolutely not," he kept saying. "Absolutely not."

That afternoon, there was a brief news conference on the local TV station. They gave out a number for people to call if they'd seen anybody matching Tracy's description. They also said they had some important information they were unable to disclose, but we never found out what that information was.

By the time it got dark, when Tracy still hadn't shown up, the police interviewed every single guest at the hotel, and the staff as well. The next day, they went to every car rental agency, ticket office and travel bureau in town. They checked all the local hospitals, ministers, churches and counseling centers. We were supposed to be flying back to Lansing that night, but Dad called the airline and changed our flight, which meant we missed a day of school.

In the hotel, they searched every guest room, every kitchen, even the elevator shafts and crawl spaces. They taped off the entrance and wouldn't let people in or out. They were even checking people's car trunks. That night, they started a full-scale search. The mountain rescue team was called in, and they drafted all available ski patrolmen and volunteers. They spent the whole night searching the mountain with helicopters and bloodhounds. The dogs were given Tracy's sweater to sniff. Later, we learned they were cadaver dogs.

The next day, in the middle of the afternoon, the search was called off. The cops said they'd done everything in their power, and there was nothing more they could do. Unbelievably, we flew home to Michigan without her. I don't know how we could have done it, but we did. I sat next to Dad on the plane, in what would have been Tracy's seat.

Jason was sitting behind us. He put his head against the crack between Dad and me, and said he remembered watching a TV show about missing people, and they said a woman who goes missing without her purse has zero chance of being found alive.

"Thanks a lot, Jason," said Dad.

When they finally found Tracy's body, they discovered than she'd been murdered less than an hour after we last saw her.

Everyone said that was something to be thankful for, but I didn't see why.

3. Cheryl

After my divorce was final, I moved into a trailer in a little place called Murdock, right across the river from downtown Baton Rouge. It might sound strange after what happened, but I still think of that time fondly. Partly, I believe, it was simply relief at being on my own, with the Mississippi River between Les and me. I didn't mind living in the trailer. I called it my tin can cottage and painted everything in the brightest colors I could find. I raided thrift stores for fabric and little knickknacks, the kinds of things I loved but Les couldn't stand. I made yellow curtains for the windows, and grew red geraniums in planters outside.

The trailer park was spitting distance from Highway 1, but the traffic didn't bother me, and if you faced out back like I did, you might as well have been in the country. There was a stretch of scrubby woodland back there where I'd seen rabbits and, once, a deer carcass with all its flesh missing. There was nothing left but bones and fur. It was a young fawn that must have fallen into a crevasse, broken its legs, and, unable to climb back up, died and rotted there, all alone.

I wonder what went through its mind?

One night, I heard a strange noise under the trailer and the next morning I found four stray kittens beneath the front steps. I began leaving them a handful of scraps every morning in an old margarine bowl. Soon they were greeting me at my front door, asking for their breakfast, and before long it was hard to stop them from slipping through my legs into the trailer whenever I left for work. Finally I gave up and took them in. Three girls and a little guy. I named them Bashful, Sleepy, Happy and Doc. Doc was the male of the bunch. He was black with white tuxedo gloves and boots, and a thin white mustache just above his upper lip. Bashful was a very fluffy grey and pink calico, and Happy and Sleepy were twins, striped in the same pattern except one was brown on white, and the other white on brown. They stayed with me for six months while I saved up to get them them all neutered, then I was lucky enough to find a home for all four of them, with a lady who looks after people with Alzheimer's disease.

I'd taken a job as a house cleaner with a real estate agency in Baton Rouge, cleaning out their properties after the renters had left. I was hoping to go into business myself, but I needed to get back on my feet first, and the work wasn't bad. The manager, a lady called Angeleen, called me every Friday and told me which days she'd need me the following week. Sometimes I had to work every day, sometimes just two or three days. Each day it was a different place, and the properties were usually pretty messed up. It would take me all day to get them clean. Angeleen knew I was a hard worker though, and she left me to work at my own pace, playing the radio or listening to the TV. Plus, anything left in the properties was considered trash, and I picked up some interesting leftovers. People abandoned all kinds of things they just couldn't be bothered to pack—books, cookware, bed sheets, a CD of Irish harp music, a set of ivory napkin rings.

Angeleen was my only friend. We talked a lot. She told me my experiences with Les had made me jaded about men. She said I needed to learn there are good men in the world, and they're not all like Les. But I know that. I know lots of good men. It's just the ones I got to know haven't turned out to be so good. Even Les seemed good at first. Turned out he was mean as a pig.

Angeleen said I'd fallen on hard times and I needed to remember the old days, when I was living on the other side of the river. She said if I thought about those days, it would be a way of reminding myself I've been on my feet before, and I'll be back on my feet again. But I told her, that's not the way I see it. The way I see it, I'm better off now. I got nothing from Les but trouble, and he ended up costing me a hell of a lot more than he was worth. As far as I was concerned, things weren't so bad here in Murdock.

The trailer next to mine in the park was a double-wide with a deck, owned by a young couple. The woman was small, cute, and curvy with dark hair in a short bob. She drove a black Mustang and played the radio at full blast. The first time I saw her, out of the blue I thought to myself: That girl is cursed.

Mustang Girl spent most of the day talking on the phone, and she liked to smoke and pace around while she talked, so she was out on her back deck a lot. Since her deck was right next to my front steps, I heard every word, whether I wanted to or not, and believe me, sometimes I heard things I'd rather not have heard. Sometimes she was out there all day. The moment she hung up, the phone would ring again.

I heard so much that I couldn't help being curious about her. She was one of those people that always seemed to be on the edge of a crisis, trying to seem upbeat when she was stuck in a tragic rut. Eventually I realized she didn't have any friends. All that time on the phone she was talking to her Mom, her gay friend Brad, or her husband, who called her four times every day minimum. I rarely saw him. He left early in the morning and got back late. At about five o'clock every day, Mustang Girl would come out onto her deck, empty her ashtray into a baggie and take it over to the dumpsters. I guess she was hiding it from him. It reminded me of the way I used to be with Les, hiding things, getting antsy when I knew he was on the way home. It's not a good way to live.

The two of them fought all the time. One time, on the phone, I heard her say she was going for coffee with Brad, and the husband must have really cursed her out, because she called her Mom in tears. She was pacing up and down, shaking and smoking.

"It's the same every day," she said. "I wake up getting cursed at because something isn't washed. As soon as he comes home, it's you motherfucker, you've been sitting on your goddamn ass all afternoon cause your ass is too lazy to go to work and you haven't done a motherfucking thing in this house. I try to tell him, I've been studying for a quiz, and he's all shut your fucking mouth, bitch."

Les had been the same. I remember the first time he hit me. It was before we were even engaged. We'd been fighting about something, I can't remember what. In those early days, I'd argue back and try to make him see things from my point of view. That hadn't lasted long.

I was getting my coat to leave and he said I gave him the stink eye, though if I did, I didn't mean anything by it. He punched me right in the nose. I remember everything going dark, then a fountain of deep red blood raining down on his kitchen floor. Needless to say, ten minutes later I was down on my hands and knees with a bucket cleaning it up.

As Mustang Girl kept reminding her Mom on the phone, she'd been married for less than a year, and she and her husband fought every night. I'd hear him start yelling at her within five minutes of getting back from work. There was always something she'd forgotten to do—pick up his medicine, wash his bowling shirt. He cursed her out constantly. Still, they'd give each other a long kiss goodbye in the morning, and she called him "baby" on the phone. It gave me chills to hear her.

One evening, not long after Christmas, I was watching the Miss Universe evening gown competition when I heard yelling and screaming outside. I turned down the volume on the TV and went to the window. The husband was dragging her out of their trailer by her hair. He pulled her off the back deck then smashed her head up and down on the hood of his truck. Feeling shaky, I closed the curtains and went to call the cops, but it was all over before I'd even got to the phone, and I suddenly felt stupid for sticking my nose in their business. I should have called anyway.

When I went to bed that night I had a slight headache. The next morning, it came on hard, and I had to call Angeleen and tell her I wouldn't be coming in to work. I took one of my pills, went back to bed, and fell into one of those strange states on the border of fever. It wasn't entirely unpleasant. Thoughts would move through my mind in a slow parade, without stopping or even slowing down. For some reason, I thought of the young deer that had fallen into the crevasse. It reminded me of a unicorn skull that Les bought for me one time at the Renaissance Faire. One of its fangs was missing, and it had been discounted.

"He stabbed me with a barbecue fork." I was woken up by Mustang Girl, pacing her deck and talking on the phone. I lay there listening, half conscious. "You can see the mark on my leg," she said. For some reason, she seemed strangely elated. "I said if he did anything like that again I was going to move back home. He knows I mean it this time. He's taking me out tonight. Pancho's. It's a Mexican Buffet. You can eat as much as you want. Including hot wings."

I slept through the rest of the day and night, and the next morning I felt better and got up and made myself some coffee. Mustang Girl, it seemed, was still upbeat. From my kitchen window, I saw her come outside in her pajamas to kiss her husband goodbye. Then she went back into the trailer and returned to the deck ten minutes later, still in pajamas and slippers, but with a sweater on top, and a poncho wrapped over that. It was January now, and chilly in the mornings. She sat down on the back steps of the deck, put down her mug of coffee, lit a cigarette then picked up the phone. I turned away from the window.

"Hey babe," I heard her say. "I got an interview … At the hospital … Two o'clock. What do you think I should wear?"

I poured out my own cup of coffee and added cream. Mustang Girl drank hers black. I heard her talking to her husband, then Brad. "I'm coming into John Mason Hall to pay my fees," she told him. "How great is that?"

I had a bad feeling in my stomach. She was never normally this happy. It didn't feel right.

I had to go and clean a house in the Garden District that day, over two thousand square feet, according to Angeleen, so I couldn't hang around. I left the trailer park just before nine. Distracted, I almost hit a yellow car turning off Highway 1, and I was so freaked out I slammed my palm on the horn, even though it was completely my fault.

It was a long day. I got back around six, and noticed Mustang Girl's car parked in her husband's spot, right beside the deck. She often parked there during the day, but she'd always go and move it before he got home, so he could park his truck outside the trailer when he got back. I went inside, washed, changed and put a steak on the grill for supper, and suddenly there were police sirens everywhere and flashing lights outside the window. I opened the front door. Mustang Girl's husband was sitting on the deck with his head in his hands. Five or six cops were wandering around, their radios buzzing, and the neighbors were gathering at a distance.

I stood there watching for a couple of minutes. Soon, an ambulance arrived and the paramedics went into the double-wide. A few minutes later, they brought out a stretcher with a body on it, draped in a sheet. Behind them, I saw blood running in rivulets down the walls.

One of the cops came over and told me Mrs. Vandeveer had been murdered. That was the first time I'd even heard her name. They wanted to know if I'd seen anything suspicious.

"You'd better come in," I said.

4. Valerie

Homicide Report

On Wednesday, May 8, 1963, at approximately 19.30, I was at the Western Avenue station when I was contacted by Sgt. Williams and told of an apparent homicide at 645a College Road in East Bay, Cambridge, between College and Mount Wilson. I drove at once to the scene. Upon arrival, I met Officer Paul James and Officer Joseph Lynch, who had responded to the original radio call. The residence was a large apartment complex just outside Williams Square. I was familiar with the building, and I knew it to be inhabited mostly by students and artists. There appeared to be no security at the front gate or anywhere in the building.

Upon entering the apartment I initially viewed the body of a naked white female lying directly in front of the door on a sofa bed in the southwest corner of the room with her head and feet pointing in the south north direction, respectively. The decedent was lying on her back with her legs spread out, her head turned to the right, and her arms tied behind her back. Her head was tilted to the right, facing the west wall.

A lace shawl was draped over her head and shoulders, covering them from view. A brief examination of the body disclosed a ligature around the neck consisting of a nylon stocking and a white scarf or handkerchief tied together, and a second ligature around the wrists. Each wrist had been individually tied. A great deal of blood was present.

A cloth had been stuffed in the victim's mouth, and a second cloth placed on top of the first. I later learned that these had been removed in order to ascertain that the victim was no longer breathing. I checked for a heartbeat or pulse, but found neither. I lifted the fabric covering the head and neck, and discovered that the neck appeared to be disjointed. There were many puncture wounds in the breast area from which massive bleeding had occurred. Bleeding also appeared to have occurred from the ears, with clotting in the right ear. The body was relatively warm to the touch, and the eyes were glassy and pupils dilated. There were signs of a very violent struggle. The bed was in disarray, the sheets and pillows were soaked with blood, and the victim's bloodstained housecoat was lying on the floor beside the bed.

I noted that the one of the windows behind the victim's body was open slightly and the curtains drawn. A lamp had been overturned and the bulb was smashed. The shade was spotted with blood. There were blood spatters on the walls, windows, furniture, and even the ceiling. The whole room gave the impression of great disorder and disarray. A second room, containing a piano, seemed largely untouched. In the kitchen of the apartment was found the murder weapon, a large knife with a serrated edge.

I supervised the crime scene investigation, then closed the scene and left the residence at approximately 23.30.

Discovery of the Body

Mr. Albert Sheldon, 33, a music teacher, first discovered the body and called the police. He identified it as his friend Valerie Kliebert, 23. Mr. Sheldon said that upon returning home that evening, he discovered a note from Mrs. Margaret Cavendish, the organist at the Universal Truth Church in Back Bay, about five blocks from the victim's home in Cambridge. In the note, Mrs. Cavendish expressed her concern that Miss Kliebert had been absent from choir practice that morning. Consequently, Mr. Sheldon, who lived nearby and had a key to Miss Kliebert's apartment, let himself in at about 19.00. After removing the two cloths from the victim's mouth and ensuring that she was no longer breathing, Mr. Sheldon called the police from the apartment at 19.06.

Autopsy Report

After I briefed him with the available information regarding the crime scene and the victim, Dr. Hall conducted the autopsy. He discovered that the victim was well developed and well nourished, and had been extensively traumatized. The scalp was covered in dark hair, and no scalp trauma was identified. The eyes were green and the pupils equally dilated. The teeth were in good repair. There was no jewelry present.

Dr. Hall stated that the victim had eaten a "large meal" within 2–3 hours prior to her death. He was unable to state positively what kind of food was consumed but stated that it might have been meat and potatoes.

The cause of death was determined to be massive exsanguination from stab wounds. Dr. Hall said there were four horizontal incised stab wounds to the throat, two on the right side and two on the left, like "parallel gill slits on a fish." He said that an additional seventeen stab wounds formed a "bull's-eye" pattern around the victim's left breast, and one of these—directly to the heart—was the fatal wound. Dr. Hall stated that the ligature around the neck was "decorative" rather than fatal. The victim had been raped by neither man nor object, nor sexually assaulted, nor were there any spermatozoa present in her body. It was estimated that she had been dead approximately 48-72 hours and had probably been killed late Sunday evening or Monday morning.

Hair and blood samples as well as fingerprints were taken from the victim by Dr. Hall and turned over to Detective Johnson. In addition, Johnson took custody of the victim's housecoat, which he removed from her apartment.

Interview with Albert Sheldon

On Thursday, May 9 at 10.10, I conducted a personal interview with Albert Sheldon, who identified himself as a "close friend" of the deceased. Mr. Sheldon informed me that Miss Kliebert was studying to be an opera singer and had planned to try out for the Metropolitan Opera in New York that year. He said she was a member of the Universal Truth Church Choir, and also played the organ in the church, and she was also a member of the Sojourner's Temple choir. Mr. Sheldon said he had known Miss Kliebert for six years, and they had attended the Boston Academy of Music together. He added that they were currently both members of the Celebration Singers, a singing group that gives recitals at the Isabella Stewart Gardner Museum and other places.

When asked to characterize Miss Kliebert, Mr. Sheldon said she was kindhearted, friendly, pleasant and a "good listener," though she could be rather reserved at times.

When asked about her male acquaintances, Mr. Sheldon reported that she took voice lessons once a week from an instructor in Harlow. He said she did not have a boyfriend, but had mentioned a man called "Lonnie" in one of her classes. Mr. Sheldon said Miss Kliebert told him she recently had to "fight him off" on a date, and the following week he proposed to her. Mr. Sheldon said Miss Kliebert seemed very disappointed about this as she had liked "Lonnie" initially, but found him too "sexually demanding" and she "did not want to have sex with him." Mr. Sheldon said that Miss Kliebert had told him she was also involved with a middle-aged married man, a college professor who had some kind of association with television. The professor had told Miss Kliebert he wanted a "femme fatale" type to star in one of his productions. When Miss Kliebert suggested she would like to play the part, the professor said she was "not the type he had in mind." Mr. Sheldon did not know what had happened after that, but he said Miss Kliebert had told him the professor was married and wanted her to "commit hara-kiri with him," because he saw no future in their relationship. Mr. Sheldon said the professor was an "odd man" who would talk to her about "strangling" and "the art of seduction."

The interview was concluded at 11.10.

Interview with Next of Kin

Mr. and Mrs. Max Kliebert of Antrim, North Carolina, were informed of their daughter's death on Thursday, May 9. I interviewed Mrs. Zelma Kliebert in her home on Friday, May 10, at 14.25.

Mrs. Kliebert informed me that her daughter had moved to Boston in 1955 to study opera, and graduated from the Boston Academy of Music in 1959. Mrs. Kliebert added that, despite a hearing impairment that made it necessary for her to wear a hearing aid, her daughter was a talented mezzo-soprano and intended to sing with the Metropolitan Opera. According to Mrs. Kliebert, from 1959 to 1962 her daughter had worked as a music therapist at the Rudolph E. Shenkman School, a facility for retarded children in Arcus, Mass. She left this position when she was accepted into the master's program in rehabilitation counseling at East Bay College, at which point she began spending two days a week interning with patients at the Chadwick State Hospital. Mrs. Kliebert said that her daughter was very practical, and if her opera career did not work out, she wanted to have a profession to fall back on. At the time of her death, she was working on a master's thesis entitled "Some Factors Pertaining to the Etiology of Male Homosexuality." Mrs. Kliebert added that her daughter was very involved with the children at the hospital, and that they would come to her home for food and a place to stay after they had been discharged. She said her daughter would help them in every way she could.

When asked about her daughter's personality, Mrs. Kliebert described her as "sensitive and emotional." She said that she felt her daughter was "too kind and trusting," and let too many people into her apartment whom she did not know, including "kooks" and mental patients for whom she seemed to be a magnet, according to her mother.

When asked about her daughter's relationships with men, Mrs. Kliebert said her daughter had been married in the past, but it had not worked out. She said the marriage had been a secret at the time, and her daughter had confessed some years later, adding that the marriage had been a failure because the man turned out to be a homosexual. He was also a Catholic, and Miss Kliebert was Jewish. She said she felt as though this man had been "warped" by his mother, who was overly protective.

Interview with Sabrina McSwain

I interviewed Sabrina McSwain on Monday, May 13 at 14.00. Miss McSwain identified herself as a "close friend" of the deceased. She reported that they had been friends for about eight months, after meeting in the Universal Truth Church Choir. Miss McSwain said she last saw Miss Kliebert on Sunday, May 5 after the noon service had ended. She also mentioned that, after a recent musical event, a group photograph had appeared in the newspapers that depicted Miss McSwain, Miss Kliebert, Miss DeVaughn, and another member of the choir. She said that shortly after the photograph appeared, the three women began to receive mysterious obscene telephone calls.

When asked about Miss Kliebert, Miss McSwain described her friend as "highly strung," "easily upset" and "someone who found it hard to say no." She added that Miss Kliebert was also very popular and had many friends, but she often found herself in the situation of "mothering" people and caring for them rather than being considered as an equal. Miss McSwain said that Miss Kliebert often got involved with the patients at the hospital she worked at, sometimes feeling "emotionally and spiritually drained" by their needs, but added that she was not the kind of person who was able to say no to anyone who wanted help. Miss McSwain described her friend as "very intense."

When asked about male acquaintances, Miss McSwain said that

Miss Kliebert always went around in a threesome with a female friend, Martha DeVaughn, and a male friend, Clarence Howland. These two were apparently her closest companions. They would sometimes accompany her to choir practice, and they would usually eat supper together in the evening before going out. Miss McSwain observed: "They were like a threesome." She added that she was aware of a former romantic relationship between Miss Kliebert and Mr. Howland, but Miss Kliebert had told her that Mr. Howland was basically homosexual and had male lovers, and the relationship between them had become one of friendship. Miss McSwain said that Miss Kliebert had informed her that she wanted to find a man who was "strong." Miss McSwain said that Miss Kliebert was tired of "weak" men who "unloaded all their problems" onto her.

The interview was concluded at 15.15.

Interview with Miss Martha DeVaughn

On Tuesday, May 15 at 10.15, I interviewed Miss Martha DeVaughn, who described herself as Miss Kliebert's "best friend." Miss DeVaughn said she had last seen Miss Kliebert on Sunday, May 5, which, according to the autopsy, was probably the night of her death. Miss DeVaughn said she had met Miss Kliebert at about 21.00 at a restaurant close to Miss DeVaughn's apartment in Brookline. Miss DeVaughn said she "chatted" with Miss Kliebert and "shared some drinks." Miss DeVaughn reported that Miss Kliebert was in a "good mood" because her opera rehearsal had gone very well (she was rehearsing an important role in the opera *La Traviata*). Miss DeVaughn said they left at about 23.00 and Miss Kliebert walked to her car, parked on Hidden Hill Road, where she chatted with Miss DeVaughn for "another ten minutes" before she left and drove back to East Bay.

When asked about Miss Kliebert's character, Miss DeVaughn admitted she felt Miss Kliebert was not careful enough. Miss DeVaughn observed that Miss Kliebert was from a small town, and consequently was too kind and trusting of strangers. Miss DeVaughn said that Miss Kliebert let people come and go too freely and did not take adequate precautions. She said Miss Kliebert did not lock her apartment door. She said Miss Kliebert would invite "mental patients" into her home, as well as the homosexual men she was interviewing for her thesis. Miss DeVaughn recalled that in January, the water pipes in Miss Kliebert's apartment had frozen and burst, and, as a result, the ceiling of her living room had collapsed. Miss DeVaughn had encouraged Miss Kliebert to move into Miss DeVaughn's apartment while the repairmen were working, but Miss Kliebert replied that she did not mind the construction.

When asked about Miss Kliebert's male acquaintances, Miss DeVaughn said that Miss Kliebert had many male admirers and dated frequently, but she was finding it difficult to meet a man she really cared for. Over the last few months, Miss DeVaughn said, Miss Kliebert had been dating a middle-aged college professor, but she appeared to be more interested in a man called "Lonnie" who was in one of her classes at Bay College. Miss DeVaughn said Miss Kliebert had described "Lonnie" as "tall, dark and handsome." Miss DeVaughn said that Miss Kliebert had initially thought that "Lonnie" was shy, but it later turned out that he believed Miss Kliebert was in a relationship with Mr. Howland, who was her constant companion at the time. Miss DeVaughn said that when "Lonnie" finally asked her to get a coffee with him at the Student Union, Miss Kliebert was "thrilled." However, when Miss DeVaughn talked to Miss Kliebert again, Miss Kliebert said that "Lonnie" had taken her out for dinner and had a lot to drink. Miss Kliebert told Miss DeVaughn she was very disappointed and said, of "Lonnie," that she basically had to "fight him off." The following week, "Lonnie" proposed to Miss Kliebert and Miss Kliebert broke up with him. Miss Kliebert told Miss DeVaughn that she did not think that "Lonnie" was serious, adding that "he makes too many demands on my femininity and I just don't know him that well." She thought he was just trying to get into bed with her and had no other interest in her beyond sex.

The interview was concluded at 11.00.

Confession

On May 25, Daniel Razo, 28, confessed to the murder of Miss Kliebert. Mr. Razo had been a longtime resident of the Shenkman School, where Miss Kliebert had worked, and he was currently working as a busboy at a nearby restaurant. Mr. Razo had a police record for being a Peeping Tom and making lewd overtures to women in public. Mr. Razo would apparently stand on the street ogling women and inviting them to get in his automobile. He was finally arrested while attempting to look under a door in a women's restroom in the Mount Wilson hospital.

Mr. Razo claimed that on the evening of May 5, he went to Miss Kliebert's apartment shortly before midnight and Miss Kliebert let him in. He said they chatted while Miss Kliebert worked at her typewriter on her thesis. Mr. Razo claimed he stabbed Miss Kliebert fifteen times with a kitchen knife, then put a gag in her mouth and a cloth over her head. Mr. Razo stated that he had gotten blood on his shirt and pants, and that he had discarded them in a trash can outside the apartment building at College and Mount Wilson. Mr. Razo was informed that his confession contained a number of discrepancies, and he was released from custody.

On May 29, Mr. Razo was killed in a swimming accident when, attempting a high dive off a bridge, he landed in shallow water and hit his head on the ground.

Respectfully submitted,

Detective E. J. William,
East Bay Police Department

5. Nancy

The honorable Brian J. Marcus had a reputation as a soft touch when it came to second chances, but third chances? Cohen didn't think even Marcus would be foolish enough to show sympathy for a criminal who'd already been arrested twice—arrested and then released, mind you—for the same offence.

He realized some people thought it wasn't a serious crime to solicit men in public, but then not everybody had seen the damage it could do. Cohen had seen that damage close-up.

This woman Nancy Lovato was no spring chicken if her mugshot was anything to go by, but Cohen knew it seldom was. He'd seen how these whores could fix themselves up, turn themselves into Catholic schoolgirls, all fresh and clean and desperate for just one last chance. He'd often thought things would be different if the judge had to sit there looking at the mugshots rather than the women themselves, smiling and simpering in their starched white suits.

"Your honor," Cohen began. "On the evening of the ninth of August 1986, the defendant was arrested by Officer Darren Miller of the

Newport Police Department and charged with soliciting sexual activity. Officer Miller reports that when searched, the defendant was found to be in possession of a bag that contained a measurable amount of crack cocaine."

He paused and took a sip of water. Now, Miller was a good cop, a real cop. Miller knew what was what. The "measurable amount of crack cocaine" had actually been a baggie, but Cohen refused to say that word. *Baggie.* It diminished the offense. It was a goddamned bag, is what it was.

"The defendant was charged," he continued, "with soliciting sexual activity, misdemeanor possession of a controlled substance, and possession of an open container of alcohol." A forty-ounce King Cobra, he assumed. It was either that or an Olde English. "The defendant filed a motion to suppress, arguing that police lacked reasonable suspicion to conduct the initial search." He paused. "This motion was denied," he said, making the emphasis clear, though he knew Schonmayer would try to bring it up again. "Would the court like Officer Miller to come forward?"

"Sure. Why not?" said Marcus.

What an asshole, thought Cohen. Still, there were worse judges than the Honorable Brian Marcus. There was a lady judge in the fourth district who looked like a cheerleader. Cohen had seen her on the court steps. She wore pink lipstick, chewed gum and tied her hair back in a ponytail. He'd heard that she sometimes even came to court directly from the gym, sweaty, with her leotard under her robe. He didn't doubt it. That's the way things were going. Marcus might seem informal, Cohen thought, but compared to some, he was goddamned hardcore.

Miller was sworn in, then Cohen asked him to tell the Court why he'd arrested the defendant. It was always his strategy to call her "the defendant" rather than using her actual name. Miller called her "the defendant" as well. They'd been through this part five or six times already, and Cohen had told him exactly what to say. His testimony was word perfect.

"I saw the defendant soliciting on East Astoria Avenue, a well-known venue for prostitution," read Miller, looking at his notes. "When I addressed her, she asked me if I was quote looking for a date unquote. She had the distinct odor of alcoholic beverage present on her breath. Her eyes were bloodshot and watery and her balance appeared unsteady. Observing that her faculties were impaired, I arrested her and charged her with soliciting sexual activity and transported her to the police station on Central Avenue."

Cohen could hear the woman sighing in protest and jingling something—bracelets, probably—but he resisted the temptation to look at her. Miller had told him she was a crackhead, and a crazy one at that, but then, weren't all crackheads crazy?

"Did you recognize this person?" he asked Officer Miller.

"Yes," said Miller, flicking his notepad closed, ready for his favorite line. "I recognized her as a known prostitute."

There were no questions, and they went straight to Schonmayer. That ambulance-chasing douchebag, thought Cohen. Whenever there was a hooker on trial, it was always Schonmayer for the defense. Cohen wondered if they paid him in sex. Sometimes he'd joke about it, but in private, he thought it was a genuine possibility. It happened. You wouldn't have to pay tax on it, after all. And some of Schonmayer's hookers were pretty hot. They weren't all skanky-looking crack whores, though most of them were. This one was, for sure.

Schonmayer now had the floor.

"Your honor, I'd like to bring Nancy forward," he said.

Marcus leaned over his dais as the woman stepped up to the stand.

"Ms. Lovato," he said. "Hi."

"Hi!" she said, brightly.

"This is the third time you have been arrested on prostitution charges, is that correct?"

Cohen was surprised; it looked as though Marcus had actually read the file for once. Even better, he didn't call her "Nancy." He tried not to look at the woman but he couldn't help giving her a quick glance. As he expected, she looked nothing like her mugshot, which was a doozy. Today, she was dressed in a high-necked blouse and goddamned *glasses*, for Christ's sake. Still, she wasn't aging well, and you could tell from her skin and teeth she used crack.

"Yes sir," she replied. "But this time I was just walking my dog."

Cohen suppressed a smile. Right, lady, he thought. Just walking your dog. On East Astoria at two A.M. In a miniskirt and boob tube. In September.

"You were walking your dog?" asked Judge Marcus.

"Yes sir."

"On East Astoria?"

"Yes sir," she said. "That's where I live. Right off East Astoria."

"This was in the middle of the night?"

"No sir. It was about ten, ten-thirty. That's when I usually take my dog out for her last potty break before bedtime."

Potty break. Cohen cursed silently. They'd been through all this in the motion to suppress, goddammit, which Marcus had already dismissed. Didn't he remember reading it, for Christ's sake? Chances are he got his staff attorney to read it, which is why he didn't remember the part about the dog. Still, at least the staff attorney had been smart enough to dismiss it. No surprise there. Plenty of staff attorneys were a hell of a lot smarter than the judges they worked for. But still, thought Cohen, now she'd brought up the goddamned dog, they were going to have to go through it all again. It was all just a goddamned waste of everybody's time and money.

Marcus had put on his glasses and was shuffling through the papers on his desk.

"Your honor," Cohen reminded him. "This was all in the motion to suppress, which you denied."

Marcus looked up.

"Was the dog mentioned in the police report?"

"No, your honor." Cohen sighed.

"What kind of dog was it?"

Jesus Christ, he thought. What the hell does it matter what kind of dog it was?

Lovato, on the stand, lit up. "She's a Chiweenie," she said.

"A Chi-what?" The judge peered at her over the top of his glasses.

"A Chiweenie," repeated the woman. "A Chihuahua and dachshund mix. I have a picture. Would you like to see her?"

"No thank you ma'am. I'm sure she's just adorable."

A *Chi-weenie*, thought Cohen, with disgust. A designer dog. Where did a crack-addicted hooker find enough money to buy a designer dog? Those things weren't cheap. His daughter had been after one for a while. If she wanted a puppy, he'd told her, then she could go and pick one out from the pound. There are plenty of decent mutts that need a home. No need for people to go breeding freaks.

"So what happened to this dog when you were arrested?" asked Marcus.

"My girlfriend Monica took him," Lovato replied, pointing to her friend who'd come to court with her. Probably another hooker, Cohen thought. He knew they usually worked in pairs.

"She was there as well?"

"She's my roommate. She saw the cop come over and arrest me, and she came and took Lola and looked after her for me until I got back from the police station."

Why, thought Cohen, the woman's a goddamned saint.

"Alright," said the judge, taking off his glasses. "And they found crack cocaine in your purse?"

"Yes sir," said Lovato. "But they had no right to search me."

Cohen couldn't let that pass.

"Officer Carr was simply enforcing the law," he stated, looking at the judge, not at the woman.

"Well, we're not here to discuss whether or not he had the right to search you," said Marcus. "That motion was dismissed. We're here now to talk about your sentence. Alright then. Mr. Cohen, you may proceed."

Cohen smiled and directed his gaze steadily at the judge. At least Marcus hadn't gone off about different dog breeds, he thought, and how his wife's King Charles Spaniel had almost won "Best in Show."

That's what Judge Disterhaupt would have done. Disterhaupt was even worse than Marcus when it came to whores. Older than Marcus, too. Should have retired five years ago, and he was still going strong. There were a lot of worse judges out there than Marcus. Still, Cohen was starting to get the sense that this case in particular was a losing battle.

"Your honor," he began. "I would like to point out that the defendant has been convicted of two offenses prior to this one, both of which involved soliciting. She has also previously been arrested for the possession of crack cocaine, for which she spent only five days in jail." *Sentenced by you, Marcus, you spineless fuck.* "She has a long history of alcoholism and drug use, and is currently unemployed and has no fixed address. I believe she has shown no improvement in her illegal and immoral behavior, and I would request that she be given a custodial sentence." *Request.* Why should he have to *request* it? If this were really about justice, he wouldn't have to *request* jail time—it would be goddamned mandatory.

Cohen returned to his seat and sat down. He could tell it was too late. It was a lost cause. That little interchange about the dog—it had softened Marcus's heart. He could tell from the way the judge's eyes had glazed over.

"Okay. Thank you, Mr. Cohen. Mr. Schonmayer?"

"Your honor, may I question the defendant?"

"Go ahead," said the judge.

Maybe we'll all learn some more about *Chiweenies*, thought Cohen. His part in the case was over. There was nothing more he could do. He crossed his legs and leaned back with a sigh.

Lovato returned to the stand. This time, Cohen got a good look at her. Okay for a crack whore, he decided, but nothing to write home about.

"How old are you, Nancy?" asked Schonmayer.

"Thirty-three." He would have said forty, at least.

"Are you married?"

"Divorced."

"Any children?"

"I had a daughter, but I gave her up for adoption."

"And may I ask why you did that?"

Because she's a crack whore, you stupid fuck, thought Cohen.

"Well," said Lovato, "I lost my job and I was using drugs, and I felt that it would be better for my daughter that she would be brought up by a family that could afford to look after her. I didn't think I should be bringing up a daughter while I was using drugs."

Meaning the social services came and took your kid, thought Cohen.

"And when did you start using drugs, Nancy?"

"Four years ago." Make that fourteen.

"And when were you first arrested?"

"Four years ago. When I was twenty-eight."

"And what happened when you were twenty-eight?"

"That's when I lost my job."

"Tell me about losing your job, Nancy."

Cohen glanced at his watch. It was almost twelve-thirty already. He wondered how much longer this was going to go on. He wondered if he could still get a Reuben sandwich at the East Side Deli, or whether they'd have sold out already. The lunch specials sold out quickly. He'd have to get there in the next twenty minutes or less.

"I was a cosmetologist in a beauty parlor."

"So, what happened?"

"They had to cut back because they were losing money. I tried to get a job in another salon, but there were no openings. That's when I first went on the streets. I couldn't pay the rent."

And of course there are only two types of jobs available, cosmetologists and whores, thought Cohen.

"So before you lost your job, you had a clean record?" Cohen winced at the cloying note of sympathy in the lawyer's tone.

"Totally," said the woman.

"You were never in any trouble at all?"

Schonmayer always coached them on this one. Never so much as a parking ticket, was what he told them to say.

"No. Not even a parking ticket."

"And Mr. Cohen said you had no fixed address. Is that correct?"

"No. I live with my girlfriend Monica. She came with me today."

That's why I said no *fixed* address, thought Cohen. He glanced at his watch again. Why was Marcus letting Schonmeyer run on and on? He was on the point of objecting, but decided he couldn't be bothered. What was there to gain by drawing it out? It would just waste more time. He sighed and resigned himself to forgoing his Reuben sandwich as the girlfriend was sworn in. A reliable friend who would vouch for them was always trouble, especially if they had a job, as this one no doubt did. He steeled himself for another defeat.

"What is your name, please?" asked Schonmayer.

"Monica."

"What is your last name, Monica?"

"McDavitt. But I go by the name Monica King." Her *nom de whore*, thought Cohen.

"And how do you support yourself, Monica?"

"I'm a cosmetologist."

"Monica, how long have you known Nancy Lovato?"

"Five, six years," she replied.

"Five or six years. Okay. And what kind of person is Nancy as far as her reliability and accepting responsibility?"

Let me guess, thought Cohen. She's amazingly reliable. And talk about responsible ... why, she's the most responsible person I've ever met. He thought of that movie, *The Manchurian Candidate*. Nancy Lovato is the kindest, bravest, warmest, most wonderful human being I've ever known in my life.

"She's very responsible. She helps out financially and she's a very kind person. She is always willing to help others."

"And if the judge were to lower Nancy's bond to an amount you could afford to post, would you make certain and assist Nancy in coming to court for whatever court appearances are required?"

"Yes sir."

Cohen sighed and snapped shut his briefcase. Keeping these crack whores off the streets was like fighting back a deluge. It was a losing battle. But he was going to keep on fighting, because nobody else in town seemed to care.

Five months later, eating his breakfast, Cohen came across an item buried deep in the local paper. The badly decomposed body found in the 6300 block of East Astoria Avenue had been identified as that of Nancy J. Lovato, a prostitute. He cut out the article and sent it to Judge Marcus in a plain brown envelope with no return address.

6. Alice

B was first brought to treatment by her father, who explained that his daughter had been experiencing panic attacks and paranoid fantasies ever since the death of her close friend, Ms. A. He said his daughter had grown progressively worse after leaving a church to which she had belonged for almost four years, and which the father referred to as a cult. Ms. B believed she was being followed by cult members, and talked incessantly about her persecution day and night. When she failed to sleep for five nights, her father and stepmother took her to a small general hospital where she was sedated. After her release, she was referred to me for treatment.

The patient was a single woman, 28 years of age, who identified herself as a model and actress, though at the time of treatment she did not work in either field, as she was afraid to leave her apartment alone. In addition to the presenting problems described by her father, B complained of constant insomnia, headaches, stomach pains, allergies, skin rashes, vague "female trouble," and many phobias—e.g., subways, darkness, black men, dogs, and traffic. She was terrified of radiation, asbestos, smog, and cancer, which, despite her knowledge to the contrary, she believed to be "contagious." She would not enter a building until she had "checked it out" for asbestos. She subsisted on savings and an allowance from her father, who was also paying for therapy in order to "help her break free" from the cult.

B was tall and attractive, with large, dark eyes and long brown hair. She normally had rather a quiet voice, but usually expressed herself clearly. She was polite and slightly obsequious at the beginning of treatment, though in later sessions her voice developed a whining, complaining tone and she could occasionally be sarcastic and contemptuous. She dressed casually and sometimes flirtatiously, in low-cut tops or T-shirts and jeans, but she was generally neat and well groomed.

Family History

The patient's biological mother died of cancer when she was three years old, and she had no memory of her, not even when looking at a photograph. Her mother became ill when B was 2, and the family decided it would be better if the girl went to live with her paternal grandparents. Two older brothers, 5 and 9, were allowed to stay home, but B did not return home until she was 5, after her father, a factory supervisor, remarried. Her stepmother is a nurse.

Her family and two older brothers all live in the greater Los Angeles area, but since they were not sympathetic to B's church, she had severed ties with them. Although she did remain in occasional telephone contact with one of her brothers, she did not speak to her father and stepmother for four years, until recently. The family was greatly upset by her newfound belief system. Her father believed her problems were all related to her involvement in the cult. He described his daughter as "dependent" and "clinging" but mentioned that she could also be optimistic, exuberant, and outgoing. He wanted her to stay in therapy until she was "normal" again. She visited my office three times a week for almost four years, often accompanied by a friend or family member who attended her in the waiting room.

The Cult

B met A, also 28, in a class offered by her church. The women became close, and moved into an apartment together shortly afterward. They had similar interests, and would sometimes visit cemeteries where there had been reports of spiritual activity. B claimed that they saw strange lights and heard "the cries of spirits." She said that on one such occasion she "felt someone breathing on her neck."

Initially, both women were "enthusiastic" members of the church, attending meetings regularly and also joining in extra activities such as suppers, picnics, and a weekly study group. They had both begun to move up the church's complex levels of hierarchy. Then a number of minor incidents occurred which led A to begin mistrusting the cult and regarding its members as hypocrites. She began dating a man who was not part of the group, and she discussed her growing doubts and ruminations with B. The women would ask each other such questions as: "What is the reason for living?" "What happens after death?" "If life ends in death, why go on living?"

Whenever I asked about the church's belief system, B would commence long, rambling digressions about "planetary systems." If I ever expressed any skepticism, she would become very defensive, pointing out to me that the church was "extremely successful," and its members included "very well-known and wealthy people."

When A began to express her doubts about the church, B said that she initially tried to think critically and to be "open-minded." She knew the church had been controversial for a long time, and she confessed that she felt drawn to controversial organizations and unusual people. She commented that over the last ten years, despite the controversy, the church had continued to grow. She felt there were a lot of falsehoods told about it, and it did not come across well in the press. At the same time, however, she admitted that those inside the church were afraid to be critical of it, and even outside detractors were criticized.

When I asked B what she had enjoyed about the church, she told me that it had helped to rehabilitate her spirit and bring out her personality, which, she said, "was smothered and hidden for so many years." She also said that the church elders made her feel highly valued because "young, attractive people are their highest priority in recruits." She said they had required her, every day, to write down a list of all her "transgressions, sins, failures and falsehoods," which she had found to be helpful, and she was required to follow a diet and perform daily exercises, which she enjoyed.

In the end, however, both women decided to leave. For various reasons, they decided the church was "not ethical." They particularly disliked the fact that church members kept confidential files and notes on all discussions. They had to memorize a lot of material "and we were not very good at memorizing." They did not, in the end, feel as though they were "bettering themselves" in the church.

The Death of A

A, also an aspiring actress and part-time model, was last seen waiting for a bus on Westwood Avenue in Los Angeles, opposite the cult's headquarters. She was observed getting into a car with two men, whom B believes were sent by the cult to abduct her. B said that A had been attracted to powerful men who "laid down the law," and she suspected her abductor might have used the badge of a police officer.

Two weeks later, A's body was found. It had been pushed out of a car near an off-ramp of the Golden State freeway, and was discovered lying in the grass with ligature marks on the neck, wrists, and ankles and puncture marks in the arms and neck. The police had a very difficult time finding any evidence because the body had been carefully washed. According to B, the police could find no hairs, fingerprints, or any other clues.

B was convinced that her friend had been "kidnapped and murdered" by members of the cult, and was terrified the same would happen to her. She frequently expressed the desire to move to "an undisclosed address," but although friends and family had offered her accommodation, she retained a deep emotional attachment to the apartment she had once shared with A, which still housed A's clothes and possessions, and she remained at this address throughout her treatment.

B described her friend A as "an angel," and seemed both devastated and obsessed by her death, which she described as "an unimaginable horror." She said A had once been involved in a "Satanist" community living in a house on 4th street, near McArthur Park, and she sometimes speculated that these people might also have been involved in her murder. Since the death of A, B was afraid to be alone. She would often be disturbed by her memories of A, such as the thought of her "meticulous, beautiful and well-kept nails."

In treatment, B talked constantly about A, becoming alternately depressed and elated. She had delusions of A being a saint or an angel watching over her from heaven, of sending her messages in the form of radio waves, cloud patterns, or words in newspaper headlines. When on the subject of A, she spoke rapidly, in a jerky manner and loud voice.

Around the same time that A's body was discovered, the dead body of a prostitute was found naked and strangled on the hillside near Westwood Cemetery. Two weeks later, the body of a 15-year-old girl was found in similar conditions, and in November, another body was discovered dumped near a golf course in Altadena. Eventually, seven more bodies were discovered in the hills around Westwood, Glendale, Pasadena and Arcadia, all killed in the same way, including two schoolgirls, aged 12 and 14, who had been missing for a week. One of the bodies was left outside a house in a street. Another was found halfway down a forty-foot cliff, and was hauled up with a crane. It seemed obvious to me that the perpetrator was the same man who had killed A, which was confirmed when a suspect was arrested in Seattle. However, B refused to believe this was the man who killed her friend, and refused to listen to the news or read the papers. She continued to believe that A had been murdered by the cult in a "copycat" crime, then thrown from a car "like garbage" so she would be believed to be a victim of the "phantom strangler." She found it significant that all the other victims were aged between 12 and 21, and A was 28.

Paranoid Fantasies

Throughout the early part of her treatment, B expressed many paranoid fantasies about A and the cult. She said, "I truly used to think everyone in the group was interested in saving the planet and helping others, but now I know they're murderers. I no longer have any idea what to believe or whom to trust." She bought a book that claimed the church was dangerous, but threw it away on the way home from the bookstore because she believed she was being followed. She now wants to escape from anyone with any cult connections, but she is afraid it is too late, and the cult will "come for" her "like they came for A." She believed members of the church had "bugged" her telephone and were watching her home day and night. She sometimes even speculated that I was being paid by the cult to report back to them after each of our therapy sessions.

Often, B would miss her appointment due to undefined illnesses. On one occasion, she had an allergic reaction to her eyelash extensions ("my eyes were itching all night, and when I woke up I looked like a raccoon"). Sometimes she would express discomfort in my office. For example, I had a picture of my children on my office desk, and she commented that they were "evil-looking." She observed more than once that there was a "bad energy" coming from the therapy couch, which, she observed, always felt "cold." She would often talk about ghosts.

For a while, B believed people were entering her apartment at night and moving things around just to frighten her. She said it might have been people from the church. Indeed, there was nothing that happened to her that she felt could not be directly related to the cult.

When speaking on this topic, she could not be derailed.

She refused to accept any medication, as she was a staunch advocate of the use of vitamins, herbs and nutritional supplements. She confessed to me that she did not believe there was such a thing as "mental illness." Instead of medication, she took short "power naps" throughout the day to boost her "energy levels."

She believed the members of the cult were trying to poison her, so she would eat only fruit and vegetables. She repeatedly claimed she needed to "remove toxins" from her system before she could begin to eat regularly again. She also claimed that cars driving by her apartment were cult members spying on her, that the trees were sending her messages, and that her bedroom ceiling was "contaminated." She was hypersensitive and claimed she could hear the coins clicking together in my pants pocket. She also claimed that wind chimes two blocks away disturbed her sleep, and she recalled that, as a baby, she could not sleep unless her bedroom door were closed, as her father's snoring kept her awake.

Treatment Progress

At first, B admitted to having "mixed feelings" about psychotherapy, since the church had strongly disapproved of it. She also admitted to suspicions about my motives.

Throughout the early sessions, we talked a great deal about A. B was obsessed with fantasies about A's death, and how much pain she must have suffered. For example, in one session she told me at great length and in minute detail a fantasy in which A was hacked to death with a machete.

During the early months of treatment, B would disappear for a week or more. Later, she told me these were episodes in which she stayed in her apartment drinking, using drugs, and eating junk food. She said these binges "came over her" when she began to feel "guilty" about A. After some time, I began to understand that she was obsessed with A out of envy and her own death wish. Part of the pleasure she got from fantasizing about A's death, I realized, was from imagining herself in similar circumstances.

In later sessions, she came to some understanding of her problems. She admitted that "I am a creative person and I always connect deeply to my feelings. It is true that I can be extreme." I explained that she needed to evolve through her mourning into a separate and related self, acquiring a unique and individual voice separate from her family, A, and the cult. She tried to do so. However, she felt deep grief at leaving these people behind.

During the third year of treatment, I began to see some progress in separation. At the beginning of her therapy, B was afraid of leaving her apartment alone. Eventually, she began attempting to do so, although she was often overwhelmed by the awareness of "being separate." Finally, as we moved toward the termination of therapy, she began to talk about A less often. Sometimes she speculated that she had killed A. At other times, she wondered if A had ever existed at all.

7. Louise

FINAL TRANSCRIPT
TIME: 11.35 AM
DATE: Sunday, April 27, 1991
VOLUNTARY STATEMENT OF: Gilbert William Hedder
AGE: 67
BORN: Cahuilla Hills, CA, August 13, 1924
EMPLOYED AT: Unemployed / Retired
I AM: Vincent John Smith, Rhyne County Police Department

VS: Okay sir, now I'm going to ask you some questions in reference to a crime scene that you witnessed this morning at the Arundel Bowling Alley at 1700 Verdejo. You may answer them or not but what you do say will be used in writing, and may be used at a trial. Okay. Do you understand?

GH: Yes.

VS: Okay, what is your full correct name, age, and address?

GH: Gilbert Hedder. G-I-L-B-E-R-T-H-E-D-D-E-R. I, um, I don't have an address right now, right now I'm staying at the shelter on Sixth. I, um, don't know the name. It's, the address is 5555 West Sixth.

VS: And that's, um, transitional housing?

GH: It's … right, a shelter, right, but I'm not homeless. I've got a … a room there with a hot plate and a small fridge and, um, my bed.

VS: Okay. I understand. And, so, um, how long, how long have you lived at that location, Mr. Hedder?

GH: Around … um, I guess, three weeks, I guess.

VS: Okay, three weeks. And before that, where did you live?

GH: Almendarez Valley.

VS: And were you also living in … um, a homeless shelter in Almendarez Valley?

GH: Well, um, I was, I was, I was originally on the wait list for Section 8 housing, um, they were supposed to give me housing but I got arrested and they said I wouldn't get housing with a record, so that's, so that's when I moved out here. I was going to try for Section 8 housing in Rhyne.

VS: Okay. So, um, why were you arrested in, in Almendarez Valley?

GH: Possession.

VS: Possession. Possession of what?

GH: Methamphetamine.

VS: And do you recall how much?

GH: Not much. I don't know. Enough to get arrested.

VS: And this was where? This was in Almendarez County?

GH: Almendarez Valley.

VS: Almendarez Valley. And this was about what, you said, three months ago?

GH: Something like that, right.

VS: And are you employed?

GH: No. I'm, um, out of a job right now, but you know, um, so is half of Rhyne County by the looks of it, I mean, you know, the whole economy's heading downhill, and, and if I had a job, I'd lose my room at the shelter, and my benefits and shit, and I'd, I'd have to start paying taxes again, and I'm too old to start again, I'm past retirement age, man. I've made it this far without a job, you know, I'm damned if I'm going to start again right at the bottom of the pile. You know, my life isn't so bad, man. I've got a roof over my head, two meals a day, and enough beer to keep me happy, just as long as I find enough cans. That's all I've got to do, find enough cans (laughs).

VS: Okay. Fine. Very good. Now, Mr. Hedder … Gilbert … is it OK if I call you Gilbert?

GH: Gil.

VS. Okay, very good. Now, Gil, so, so, early this morning you called the police, and, um, to report that you'd seen something, something unusual at the Arundel Bowling Alley at 7100 Verdejo. Would you mind telling me in your own words what you were doing there?

GH: Sure. Well, I was up early looking for aluminum cans. Sometimes I get up and go looking for cans before the trash cart gets there, you know. After a while, you know the best places to go. The secret is, you've got to get there early, I mean, *real* early, I mean, like, before daylight, that's when you find the most cans, before the trash cart gets there. I always check out the bowling alley because they sometimes have a lot of cans around there. Beer cans, you know, there's a set of dumpsters by the parking lot that are real good for beer cans. I guess folks want to carry on drinking after their … you know … after the bowling alley's closed down for the night.

VS: And will you tell me in your own words about what you saw, Gil?

GH: Um, okay, um, I was rooting around in the bushes, um, you know, the shrubbery on the edge of the parking lot, and I started to get this creepy feeling like somebody was staring at me from behind, I mean you know the hairs on the back of my neck were standing up, you know, I … um … I felt my blood run cold, and then, then … (inaudible) I saw this body on the ground. First I thought it was one of those dummies, like a store window dummy, you know, um, a mannequin, but then I went closer and I saw it was, it was a dead body.

VS: Can you describe the place where you found the body, Gil?

GH: You know … round the back of the bowling alley, there's like … a parking lot on the left side … if you're coming this way, towards it, like this … and there's like … grass, and some planters and shit next to the parking lot, and that's where it was.

VS: On the grass?

GH: Right. In the corner, on the grass, in between two of those … you know, those planters. Right on the edge of the parking lot.

VS: Did you, could you see the body from the parking lot?

GH: No.

VS: How about from the road? Would the body have been visible from the side road?

GH: Ummm … well, I don't think so. I mean, it wasn't exactly hidden, but it was like … in a corner … but if you walked over there you'd see it right away. I mean, you couldn't miss it.

VS: But only if you were walking on the edge of the parking lot?

GH: Hard to say. Depends where you were looking, I guess.

VS: Okay. Thanks, Gil. Now, okay, can you describe the body?

GH: Yeah, um, she was small, real small. First I thought she was a kid, till I saw her, um, her bush. Real skinny, you could see her ribs, she, she was real skinny. Dark hair, dark bush, but her skin was white.

VS: What about her face?

GH: You know, she was lying … like … with her head on one side … I couldn't really see her face.

VS: How close, just how close did you get to the body?

GH: Just to, to, you know, to see if she was dead. I didn't want to get that close. You know. I was pretty freaked out.

VS: Did you touch her?

GH: Um just … you know … um, to see if she was dead.

VS: Wasn't it obvious, I mean, that she was dead?

GH: Well, you say that, but um … I don't know man. I mean, I saw she was real pale, but I looked for a bullet hole and I couldn't see one … I mean, but, you know, I mean, there was no blood or nothing, and I thought … what if she was still breathing or something? But, but as soon as I touched her, um, I knew she was dead, and I knew somebody, I knew somebody killed her.

VS: How did, how did you know that she'd been killed?

GH: Well, I mean … um, it was obvious … I mean, there's nothing natural about a naked chick lying dead in the parking lot of a bowling alley.

VS: So … yes, but there was no visible sign of how she was killed?

GH: Right, I guess, I mean, I guess, um, she was, she was strangled, right?

VS: Well … um, we don't know the answer to that right now, we haven't had the autopsy results back yet, but yes, it looks that way.

GH: (inaudible)

VS: So, um, can you tell me where you touched her?

GH: I … I … um, I just put my hand on her stomach for a second, just to see if she was cold.

VS: And was she?

GH: She was real cold.

VS: We're only asking you to give us the truth, okay?

GH: I understand. I'm giving you the truth. This is the truth.

VS: Okay. Now, how long was your hand on her stomach for, Gil?

GH: Just for a second. Like I said, I mean I was freaking out. I'd just found this dead chick. You'd probably be doing the same, man, if it was you.

VS: Did you find her attractive?

GH: Shit, no. I mean, if she'd have been alive, maybe. But I just thought, shit, it's a dead body, you know I mean I didn't think about what she looked like, I'm not into dead chicks, man.

VS: So, um, you, you were close enough to touch her, but you still didn't see her face?

GH: Her head was turned … she was facing the wall. I didn't look that closely.

VS: And did you notice anything, anything unusual about the body? Anything that had been done to the body, I mean?

GH: Yeah … there was something between her legs…. Like I said, I didn't look too closely.

VS: What did it look like?

GH: I think it was … you know … (pause) like one of those things you use to clean a toilet. That thing with the … like … rubber part on the end, whatever.

VS: A toilet plunger?

GH:: Yeah. Right. A toilet plunger. I could see the rubber part.

VS: Anything else?

GH:: Not that I saw.

VS: Any blood?

GH: No, I mean, if there was any it was washed away when the sprinklers came on. I mean (inaudible) I just about shit myself, the noise they made, it fucking spooked me, man.

VS: These were the lawn sprinklers?

GH: Right. All of them. And the water hit her body, and I thought, so, that, that's going to wash away the … you know, all the fingerprints and all that shit. So I goes over to the bowling alley and I knocks on the doors, but there's nobody there. So I stays for three or four minutes in case there's somebody in back or something, but nobody came, so, so then I went to the corner of the street and called the cops from the pay phone there.

VS: What street was this?

GH: Verdejo and, um, whatever the next side street is. Weldon, maybe?

VS: And you waited for the cops to come?

GH: Right. And they, they brought me downtown, and here I am.

VS: Well, Gil, we sure appreciate all your help.

GH: No problem. (Pause). Are we finished?

VS: Not too much longer, but … um, I still need to ask you a few more questions, okay?

GH: Okay.

VS: Okay. Gil, I want you to tell me the truth. And ... okay, this is nothing to do with this woman's death, okay, we just need to know, for the record. When did you last do meth?

GH: Um ... yesterday.

VS: That was the last time? Be straight up with me, Gil.

GH: Right. 'Cause I was ... yeah, yesterday.

VS: And you're pretty ... very sure, you're certain about that?

GH: Pretty certain.

VS: So you haven't done any today? You mean yesterday, the 19th?

GH: Saturday.

VS: Saturday. Okay. The 19th. You mean, you mean the 19th, right?

GH: Right. Whatever. I don't know what the date, okay, but yeah ... whatever the date was yesterday.

VS: Yesterday.

GH: Right.

VS: And how long have you been using meth?

GH: Twelve years, more or less.

VS: Well and are you trying to quit, um, to quit that habit?

GH: (Pause) Not really, no, not at all. You know, it gives me energy, energy, excitement. Before that, it was heroin, then before that it was alcohol, and you know man (inaudible), I'm an ex-con, who's going to help me? Nobody's going to help me, man, nobody, like, nothing's going to change in my life, okay? At least if I had a house, a car, something, I might want to get straight, but I live like a dog, there's no ... um (inaudible), no incentive for me to get clean.

VS: So it's been part of your life for twelve years. That's a long time.

GH: Sure. Right. Right. It's part of my life. Makes me feel strong. Gives me energy, and when I start coming down I just want more.

VS: You've never, um, tried to get help?

GH: Are you kidding? I mean, you know, there are enough problems in this town, man. Who wants to help addicts? Everybody I know does meth, man. It's, you know, its cheap, it's easy to make. You can make it with stuff you get from the drugstore, whatever. It's the poor man's drug, anybody can make it. You don't sleep, you're up all night man, it's ... you know ... it's great.

VS: Do you do any other drugs?

GH: Sure, I've done it all, man, mary jane, crystal, coke, heroin, acid, PCP, glue, I've done everything.

VS: And you've got no, no interest in quitting, getting clean?

GH: What, you got to be kidding, why? No, no, I don't want to quit, I've given up trying to quit, man. I'm fine with it, you know ... it doesn't make me violent, I'm fine. With meth, you don't need to eat, don't need to sleep, matter of fact all your needs are taken care of, man. It's, it's, like, the drug of choice for (inaudible) ... for people like me.

VS: Okay. Well. Okay, well, I can understand that. Okay. Gil, I need to ask you something else, okay? Did you, um, did you recognize the dead woman?

GH: Not at the time, no. But while I was out there ... in the waiting room ... you know ... I was talking to the cops, and ... they told me it was this deaf chick that worked in the Budget Inn on University, and I'd been there a couple of times with some buddies, and then I remembered her, yeah.

VS: You knew her?

GH: I'd seen her, yeah, I mean you know, I didn't know her name. But I'd seen her around. Only when they told me that she used to work as a maid at the Budget Inn, and she was also a hooker, I put two and two together and remembered that I knew her ... I mean, I didn't really know her but I'd met her a couple times there at the Budget Inn. Never knew her name, though, or if I did I didn't recall it. Real nice girl, real sweet. Pretty. She was deaf, too. They told me she had a kid. I only learned that later, I didn't know it at the time, but, but like I said before, I didn't see her face, and even if I had, I probably wouldn't have recognized her.

VS: Why not?

GH: Well ... they said she was pretty beat-up.

VS: So you knew her?

GH: Not exactly. I met her once, like I said, at the motel.

VS: When was this?

GH: Must have been a couple years ago.

VS: Can you be more specific?

GH: Not really. I mean ... a couple of years ago. That's all I can say. I knew this guy, this guy Ray, he was, he was the night manager there, at the Budget Inn, I knew him from the shelter on Sixth. He lived there for a while. When business was slow and the motel was empty, Ray would, um, he would open up one of the rooms at night and some of us would get together and party.

VS: Can you be a little more specific?

GH: You know I mean we'd have some beers and party a little, watch some TV, movies or football or a porno, whatever. Invite some ladies round. That's where I met this chick.

VS: The woman whose body you found?

GH: Right.

VS: Do you remember talking to her?

GH: Sure. I remember her, yeah, because she was, she was working in the motel and she'd tell us not to make too much of a mess in the room because it was her that would be cleaning up in the morning. Like I said, she was real nice.

VS: Were you attracted to her, sexually?

GH: Sure I was. She was real cute. But I got the impression she was with this other guy.

VS: Did you know his name?

GH: No, I mean, we all called him Montana, because that's where he was from, and I got the impression they were a couple. Otherwise, sure, I'd have asked her out on a date, she was cute. Maybe a little too young for me, young enough to be my daughter. But what the hell, it would have been worth a try, just to ask her. Can't hurt to try, right?

VS: So what happened at this party?

GH: Well, like I said, this guy Ray opened up a room for us, just like a once in a while kind of thing. We were going to watch the replay of the Superbowl, so that's when it was, the day of the Superbowl a couple of years ago, I remember, because all day, all day, you know, we were trying to avoid the TV and radio, I was putting my hands over my ears when anybody started talking about the game, you know, because we didn't want to know who won. I remember this chick, because she made that comment about, about us not trashing the room, and I said, "That's OK honey, I'll take the cans," and everybody laughed, and she said, "Well, that's one less thing I'll have to pick up." I remember that.

VS: And were there any drugs at the party?

GH: Yeah, we were doing meth. We were all doing it, everybody was doing it. They still do. I still do, I mean, I get up every day and go to get my daily dose, same as everybody else. Five bucks, I can be high for half a day. It's everywhere, man, you know that. This chick did meth, and she was a hooker, right?

VS: You knew that?

GH: Not at the time, but that's what the cops told me this morning ... a lot of hookers used that place to do meth. The Budget Inn.

VS: This woman worked there as a maid.

GH: I know.

VS: So you didn't know that she was a hooker or that she did meth until this morning?

GH: Right. But it wasn't any big surprise. Like I said, everybody I know does meth.

VS: But you knew she was deaf, and that, and that she had a child?

GH: That's what I'd heard from Ray.

VS: Did you know anything else about her?

GH: No.

VS: And you, you're not lying to me now, Gil, right?

GH: I don't want to lie to you.

VS: Do you know her name now?

GH: Louise, right?

VS: That's Correct. Louise Kessler.

THIS STATEMENT consisting of __ pages signed by me is true to the best of my knowledge and belief and I make it knowing that, if tendered in evidence, I shall be liable for prosecution if I have willfully stated in it anything which I know to be false, or do not believe to be true.

Gilbert W. Hedder

8. Kayla

She wasn't clean and she wasn't pretty, but I'd have taken a bullet for that girl, and anyone who says otherwise can suck my dick. I've known Kayla at her very worst. I've seen her lying on the floor with puke in her hair, her legs covered in shit, and another man's jism all over her tits. And I still loved her. I always loved her.

Kayla was like me, a lost soul. She was born in a small suburb outside of Minneapolis and she got the fuck out. She'd been raped a couple of times, and didn't have much trust in men. The only person she truly loved was her mom, who thought she was working as a dancer. That was her plan at first. She thought it would be real fancy, dancing in a New York club. Well, she did it for a while, but it was in a strip club and the pay was shit and the guy who owned it was a fucking asshole. So Kayla figured if she was going to live off her body she might as well get good money for it. She said she'd rather be earning decent money working the street than dancing in a sleazy club for next to nothing. She didn't tell her mom what she was doing. I guess she wanted her mom to believe she was living in a fancy world.

Some people think working the streets is an easy way out, but believe me, Kayla didn't have it so easy. It took her a while to get a regular track. She'd be out there for hours in the cold and rain, pounding the pavements, hanging out at gas stations, working truck stops, never even getting a room, just climbing into the truck for a few minutes or doing it outside, behind dumpsters, wherever. The money wasn't great, either. It just about beat the strip joint, but it wasn't great. Forty dollars for a blowjob. Straight fuck fifty. Half-and-half seventy. If they went to a hotel, it was a hundred. She'd work the south side for hours, getting into fights with other girls. And the johns could be tough. They'd want to bareback, beat her up, everything. One time she got picked up by a group of cops and she had to give them all blowjobs. Her ex-boyfriend Nick Frantz got her hooked on smack, and then he got clean but Kayla didn't. First she did it now and then, for fun—she was snorting it for years—but of course in the end she got a habit, like we all did. And of course Nick got sick of her being high all the time. It was clean up or get out. After they split she got a lot worse.

Three times I helped her to get straight. It was hell. I remember coming home and she'd be sitting on the kitchen floor, unable to walk because her legs couldn't bear her weight, she was that thin. She had no appetite, and when I made her eat she'd just vomit all day, then she'd be lying on the floor moaning, covered in puke. The first time, it took her five days to get over the worst, then she felt like shit for another three weeks after that. It was still in her blood. All she could digest was milkshakes. The second time she spent three days curled up naked in the bathtub with her head in her hands. The third time, she didn't even make it two days till she started feeling like she wanted to get out of her skin. I knew exactly how she felt. I'd tried to quit myself. And watching Kayla, it all came back to me—the chills that start at the top of your head and end at the heels, the skin stinking with sweat, having to piss every two minutes and nothing comes out, constant diarrhea, shaking, chewing your fingernails, pain in your bones and muscles, pain in your fucking *blood*.

I had a serious habit myself by the time we met, and with me using, there was no chance Kayla could stay clean. The only time I got straight was in jail. I did eighteen months for robbery in the second degree, and when I came out I was clean, but in three days I was on the street and strung out again, trying to bum enough money for a bottle of wine. Getting clean is the toughest thing. I know Kayla tried hard, but she just couldn't do it. You can only do it if you're in jail or if you've got a good support network, and that is something we did not have. In the end we just stopped trying to quit. We were functional addicts. By working the streets at night, Kayla could make enough to pay our rent and pay for us to get high. I'd go out with her and wait for her when she picked up a john. Sometimes I'd wait by the car or whatever until they were done. Usually, I'd write down the license number, so if anything happened we could track the guy down. A lot of people said I was her pimp, but I wasn't her pimp, I looked out for her, I didn't work her.

Some nights she would make around six hundred dollars. Once she had four hotel dates in a night. But most of the time it was a lot less. It was hard work, and people treated her like a piece of trash. She wasn't ashamed of what she did, but she wouldn't have got into it if it hadn't been for the drugs. Kayla was smart. She could have gone to college. She could have done anything she wanted. But once she'd started working the streets, she felt as though she couldn't go back.

To me, the relationship was normal. At first I told her, if I can't take what's going on, we're either going to have to come up with a different solution or else part company. But it never came to that. I got used to it. We were like any other couple. She didn't tell me anything about what went on, and I didn't ask. I didn't care. As far as I was concerned, the less I knew, the better. We didn't think of it as sex—it was just a way of making money. Our days were organized around one simple goal: getting a fix. Scraping together enough money to score. We'd shoot up right there in the road.

At night, you wouldn't recognize Fourth Street; it was like a jungle. Some of those men were animals. Sometimes the most proper looking guys were the freakiest. I saw what they did to her. A guy stabbed her in the arm once with a pair of rusty pliers. But they weren't all bad. Truth is, there were also a lot of decent guys who worked all week long and just saved up to get laid.

She went missing on June twenty-third. We were on West Fourth Street in the Village, about four-thirty in the morning. Kayla was standing on the street, in one of her usual places, and I was on the steps. This guy pulled up in a light brown car. I didn't get a good look at him, but she told me it was okay, he was a regular and she'd be back in twenty. I didn't even write down the guy's plate number. The next time I saw her, it was on a slab in the morgue.

First I figured he'd taken her to a hotel for the night, but she didn't come back the next day, and I went up the wall. I called all the emergency rooms in the city, and then when I couldn't put it off it any more I called the cops. The guy on the phone told me I could come down to the station and fill out a missing persons report, but there was nothing they could do until she'd been missing twenty-four hours. Then I told him she'd been working on the streets. I was expecting him to say, well she's a hooker, what do you expect, there's nothing we can do. But it turned out they were pretty cool about it. When I went down to fill out the paperwork, it turned out one of the cops was a fan of Seventh Legion and had seen us last fall at CBGBs.

The next day I put all these flyers up on telegraph poles where Kayla used to work on the Lower East Side and all over the Village. They had pictures of her in the blue motorcycle jacket she was wearing on Friday night. I walked all over town and talked to everybody that knew her but nothing happened for six days. Then on June twenty-eighth, I got a call from the cops saying they'd found a body and they wanted me to come down and take a look. Then the guy said she had tattoos on her back of a purple flower and an upside-down cross, so I knew it had to be her and it was.

What happened was this. These two cops were driving on the Northern State Parkway on the Island and they saw this white truck with no license plate, and when they signaled for the guy to pull over, he took off and they got into a chase. They told me the guy was going over a hundred all the way to Escudero, where he crashed into a streetlight right in front of the post office. When the cops checked out the truck they smelled something real bad, opened up the back and there was Kayla, wrapped in a blue tarp. This fucker had been on his way to dump her body. He told the cop he'd picked her up on West

Fourth Street and driven her to this parking lot on the Island where he'd fucked her then strangled her. They said she was the second girl he'd picked up that night and he went with hookers all the time. Why he didn't strangle the other girl, Christ only knows. Maybe he was too tired. I don't know what they'll do to him. I hope he gets the fucking chair. The cop told me Kayla did not suffer. He said she would have passed out right away. He said she probably was not even aware what was happening to her. I don't know how he knows that.

Anyway, the cops got a long confession out of this psycho. He said that after strangling Kayla he drove back down to Garden City and left her body in the trunk of his mom's car while he went to the hardware store to pick up some tarp and rope. Then he went home to his mom—yes, he lived with his mom, like all psychos do. He told the cops he'd only just gotten back home when his mom wanted her car keys because she was going shopping, and off she went in the car, with Kayla's dead body wrapped up and hidden in the trunk. When the psycho's mom got back, he moves Kayla into a wheelbarrow and wheels her into the garage and then, get this, the fucker spends the next three days just working on his fucking pick-up with Kayla's body lying there in the hot garage in the middle of fucking July. The guy must have been one hell of a psycho if you ask me. Finally the smell must have got to him, because he puts her body in his pick-up and is on his way to some waste ground near Nassau when he gets into a chase with the cops. Now they tell me this guy confessed to killing seventeen other girls. First they thought he was just bullshitting, but the cop tells me they've been going round digging up bodies all round the Island.

I know her mom is going to be pissed about what Kayla was doing, but I honestly think she would have got out of it if she could have kicked her habit. She had a lot of problems but she was a fucking angel to me. I don't know if I'm going to get through this one. First I lose my band, now my fucking girlfriend. Now I've got no money for rent, let alone smack. I don't know how I'm going to get my life back together after this.

I keep remembering Kayla's twenty-first. We had a party at our place on Fourth Street. She had so many friends around then. Everybody loved her. Everybody knew about her sense of humor, but only I know how kind and sweet she was. Whatever else, she was a free spirit who lived her own life the way she wanted to and she didn't take any shit from anyone, not even me.

My mom says I haven't grieved properly and Kayla is in heaven and she thinks I'm insane and not compassionate and I'm evil because I don't care about death. I had to tell her, Mom, I don't believe in heaven so you should save your breath and not give me all this shit about Kayla's soul hovering over earth. That really set her off.

Last night I had a dream that Kayla was still alive and we were back living in the place on Fourth Street. It was winter. She went out to get some milk from the bodega and she didn't come back. I went downstairs to look for her and there was this car moving down the street in slow motion. I don't know who was driving, but Kayla was in the passenger seat and as the car went by she turned and looked and waved at me. Then she was gone.

9. Emi

She's a tiny girl, like an elf. She has dark hair and almond eyes, and she wears a yellow slip and pink ballet slippers. Her mother is stitching the last sequins on the white dress she'll wear to the World Trade Fair in Omaha, where, with two other girls, she is going to perform a demonstration of traditional dance. When she finishes school, she wants to join the Korean ballet. She's already been invited to audition. One evening in September, just after six o'clock, she leaves home to take the bus to her dance class. She waits on Conway Avenue, between Garland and Williams. The bus is late. She sticks out her thumb.

Emi's mother, Janet, has a touch of second sight. She sees things no one else can see. Sometimes, while washing dishes at the sink, she notices dark forms moving about under the trees in the yard, like the shadows of little creatures.

She told Emi not to hitchhike, and Emi said she never would, but Janet knew what she was thinking.

She was thinking, I can take care of myself.

Janet, who is divorced from Emi's father, works as a guard at an art museum just outside Berkeley. She likes the job. People ask her all kinds of questions, anything from what time does the museum open to who's her favorite artist and where can I get a calendar. She's there to deal with any issues they might have. If she can't help them, she'll direct them to somebody who can. The pay is good, and the environment is free and open. She just has to try to arrange her shift to avoid working with one certain man—a man who does nothing but talk all day about being in the Korean war and calling all the guards lazy or gay, a man who leans against the wall all day when the guards are not supposed to lean against the walls.

That night, Emi should have been home by nine. When she isn't back by ten-thirty, Janet knows she is dead. There is no question in her head—she just knows. It's as though a bomb has gone off. A mother's instinct. She waits until midnight, then calls the police. On the phone, they tell her she should try not to worry, but she's not worrying, she's certain: Her daughter is dead.

An hour later, an officer with a thick moustache drives over to take a statement.

She's dead, Janet tells him, opening the front door.

Why don't we sit down, says the officer. Chances are, she's run away from home. He takes off his hat and lifts a pile of fabric from a chair. She'll be back. Or if not, she'll write you a letter. But most likely, she'll turn up. They always do.

Emi's a good girl, Janet tells him. She'd never just leave. She was going to Omaha at the end of the month, to dance at the World Trade Fair. I've just finished her costume. Look.

The truth is, ma'am, all kinds of girls run away from home.

She's only fifteen, Janet continues. She doesn't smoke or drink. She's never had a boyfriend. She's never been in trouble her whole life until she started hitchhiking.

Hitchhiking's against the law, ma'am.

I know. I told her. But we don't have a car. It's my fault. I never learned to drive.

You shouldn't blame yourself, ma'am.

See, she's emotional, easily led. She doesn't have any experience. She doesn't realize that people take advantage of you.

I know what you mean. The policeman began to fill out a form. My daughter's the same. She thinks she's all grown up, but she's just a little girl.

I've been afraid all summer, said Janet. I said she could go as long as she promised me she wouldn't hitch a ride. She promised, but not seriously. You know, she got her first ticket this summer, for hitchhiking. She's never been in any kind of trouble before, but she's been doing it since spring. I didn't know how to stop her. I'm sure she didn't think anything could go wrong.

Trust me, ma'am, said the officer. The nicest young people run away from home today. Their folks never believe it, just like you. Chances are at least fifty-fifty your daughter's met up with some other young girls and joined a commune. The best thing you can do is to get some flyers printed with her picture on them.

At first, Janet's heart can't stand the pain. She's always been there for Emi, catching her, calming her, taking care of her when she's sick, holding her when she's got a headache. She's brought this child up so carefully, looked after her so well, and now someone has taken her away, and all that love is wasted. Janet tries not to think of it that way. She tries to remember that Emi's soul was God's to take, not hers.

It's the kind of tragedy that can tear a family apart, but Janet's family was already torn apart. It had happened years before, when her husband walked out. That was the year Emi changed. She became more outgoing, independent. Janet wondered: Why couldn't she just dance, play softball, do the things she used to do?

After her father left, Emi wanted them to move into the city. They had taken the bus there together many times, the two of them. The Castro district had been full of men standing outside the bars, watching them. Everyone was smoking pot. Janet felt as though the structure of everything was starting to break down. The previous summer, from the steps of the museum, she'd witnessed antiwar demonstrations and a gay liberation parade.

In the city, Janet and Emi would walk hand in hand along the Marina, looking out over the water to the hills in the background. They'd walk past the piers and warehouses of Fisherman's Wharf, stopping at a wooden picnic table on the waterfront to eat steamed crabs. They'd go and listen to the street musicians at the Cannery. Sometimes there was a group of banjo players, sometimes there were gospel singers—both blacks and whites together—and even a man playing the bagpipes with a hat for donations, though asking for money was supposed to be illegal. Once there had been a wonderful clarinet player, but the man accompanying her on the guitar only seemed to know one or two chords.

Take a load off Mary. That was the song that Janet remembers best.

People tell her to cherish every moment, but she wonders: What does this really mean?

She knows Emi is dead, but she is embarrassed just to do nothing. People would have found it strange, suspicious. It would have looked as though she didn't care. So she makes flyers, like the officer advised. Have You Seen This Girl? Underneath is a picture of Emi: fifteen years old, five feet tall, and ninety-three pounds. When last seen, she was wearing a white linen blouse with an embroidered appliqué, a green silk skirt, and thong sandals. It was a warm evening. The white linen had looked so beautiful next to her tanned skin.

Janet describes her as daughter as "Asian-Norwegian." She remembers a day four or five years ago when her daughter came home from school upset because one of the teachers had referred to her as Korean. Emi did not like to be described as Korean.

Don't fret. You're an exotic-looking child, her mother reassured her. Even at age eleven, she thought Emi was dangerously beautiful. The child had worn braces, and for a while, when she was young, there'd been talk of surgery for her lower jaw, but in the end it wasn't needed. According to the dentist, Emi was perfect as she was.

Soon, there are flyers all over Oakland: Have You Seen This Girl? Janet sees the picture of Emi everywhere she goes. In late October, she gets a call from a woman whose daughter remembers seeing Emi and another girl at the bus stop on Conway Avenue, between Garland and Williams. The police track down the second girl, Eunice Kim, who knows Emi from school. According to Eunice Kim, the bus was late and Emi wanted them both to hitch a ride. Eunice Kim said she wasn't allowed to hitchhike, and Emi said she wasn't supposed to either, but she did it anyway. She did it all the time, she said. It's easy, she told Eunice. Watch.

Emi stepped away from the curb and stuck out her thumb. A few minutes later, according to Eunice, a car stopped to pick her up. Emi beckoned for Eunice to join her, but Eunice shook her head.

The police ask Eunice what kind of car it was. Eunice knows nothing about cars. She has no idea. She thought it was a large one, maybe brown or possibly cream. They ask her to describe the driver, but she only caught a glimpse of him. She thinks he was a white man, but she's not entirely sure.

In February, the newspaper contains an article about hitchhiking girls going missing. Now they think someone is killing them one by one. According to the newspaper, it is probably someone you would never suspect, like your next-door neighbor. The police think he is driving around with a gun under his seat. They say we are seeing crimes today that have not happened before, new kinds of crime, people taking multiple lives with no apparent motive. To kill a little girl like Emi, what motive could you have, wonders Janet.

They interview a cop who says it's probably been going on a couple of years. They ask him what kind of man would do such terrible things, and the cop says it might be someone who tortured pets and other small animals as a child. It might be someone who feels inferior, and takes out these feelings in anger and violence. It might be someone who fears women, who feels angry and unhappy. Or it might be someone who's simply gone off the deep end. They ask him how he traps the girls, and the cop says maybe he's rigged his car in some way so they can't get out. They ask him how they plan to catch him, and the cop says it's not that easy. Once these guys start, says the cop, they can't be stopped. If this guy gets lucky, he could just go on and on until he loses interest. On the other hand, everyone makes mistakes, and maybe this guy will make one.

At the museum, they're told not to play cop, but Janet always carries a can of mace in her back pocket. She never knows when she might have to use it. Still, most of the time, nothing happens. When she started there, they made her take classes in liability, crisis management, and what to do in case of an accident, but the museum is a very peaceful place. They're supposed to keep an event log, but it's mostly blank. Sometimes people try to smoke in the hallways or steal from the shop, but nothing else. No fires, no emergencies, no art thefts, even though it's a world-class museum. Someone fainted once. Someone once had an epileptic fit. Kids run through the halls and she has to tell them to stop, and sometimes she has to tell people not to lean against the glass or touch the paintings, but that is all.

At first, Janet thinks her work will keep her occupied, but it isn't enough. Although she has plenty of friends at the museum, the staff members are supposed to alternate their breaks, so there's always someone on duty. This means she has to eat lunch alone.

She keeps out the dress Emi was to have worn to the World Trade Fair in Omaha. In late September, a year after Emi disappears, they find the dismembered bodies of two girls in the mountains. Janet packs up the dress and stores it in the basement. They want her to come in for an update on the case, but she does not return the call. My little girl is dead, she thinks, and there is nothing you can do.

Now, every morning, when her bus travels toward the Berkeley hills, she looks out at the city skyline and wonders: Is this the last thing my daughter saw?

Whenever she hears a car door slam or a trunk lid close, a horrible shudder goes through her.

She thinks God will help her, but God is not enough. Whenever Janet closes her eyes to pray, all she sees is her little Emi, turning and turning in her lacy white dress.

10. Ellen

Date: April 11, 1989

Patient Number: 004823

Supervisor: Joan Wright Lieberman, LCSW

INTAKE REPORT

I. IDENTIFYING INFORMATION

Patient Name: Ellen Patricia Watts

Occupation: Legal secretary

Age: 24

Marital Status: Single

Date of Birth: June 17, 1965

II. PRESENTING CONCERNS

Patient presented with various issues around her current life situation, reporting that she feels "depressed" and "bored, stuck in a rut." She said that, until recently, "everything was on track" and "my life was going just as I'd always planned it," but a series of unexpected events, including the breakup of a romantic relationship some time ago, have left her feeling "really sad and lonely." She feels as though her life has "gone off the rails." Patient saw a counselor very briefly in high school, but otherwise has no experience of therapy. "I never felt like I needed it. I was always fine. I don't understand what happened to me."

III. Appearance / Behavioral Observations

Patient was on time for the appointment and her body language seemed at ease. She appeared attractive and well groomed. She was dressed in appropriate clothes and displayed a shy, slightly nervous demeanor. She has brown wavy hair with blonde highlights, and was wearing hoop earrings and a necklace that appeared to be made of gold. She looked a little younger than her stated age. She seemed intelligent and articulate. Her posture was upright and she made eye contact throughout the entire session. She was fully focused on the questions that were being asked, and she answered them as well as possible.

IV. Family Background

Patient reported that she was born in Clear Lake but her parents moved to Jacksonville when she was five. She is the oldest of four children, with two brothers and one sister. She said that her parents have been married for over thirty years and they still live in Jacksonville, in the house where the patient grew up. She is "very close" to her parents. "We talk on the phone all the time." She visits them every two or three weeks. Her siblings are all still living at home. She reported that her father studied law at Jacksonville University, and now owns his own law firm. Patient stated that both her grandparents on her father's side are still alive and her grandmother on her mother's side is still alive. The patient stated that she does not recall feeling a lot of emotion when her grandfather died because she was only six years old when it happened. Patient described her mother as "totally supportive" and very helpful when it comes to personal feelings. "I have heard a lot of my friends say how much they hate their parents. I could never ask for better ones." The patient expressed that, because her mother and father are so wonderful, it will be hard for her when they pass away.

V. Health

On a scale of one to ten, the patient feels that her health is a seven or eight, despite the fact that she smokes about "half a pack" of cigarettes every day and drinks "about three glasses of wine" with dinner every night. She also drinks cocktails at the weekend. She expressed the wish that she could exercise more, but she feels that with her work and social schedule, she does not have the time to fit it in. She said, "At school, I played a sport every season. I played soccer in the fall, basketball in the winter, and softball in the spring. Now I just don't have the time." She said that she broke her collarbone when she was around three or four years old. "I did this by climbing from a chair onto a table and either fell or jumped off the table. This happened while playing with my brother." Other than that, the patient stated that there have been no problems with her health except that she is "shortsighted" and wears contact lenses. When she first moved to Jacksonville, she joined an athletic club, "The Total Gym," in Riverdale, but she said she only went there "once or twice."

VI. Education

Patient went to Wilson High School in Jacksonville. "I made mostly 'A's and 'B's, and always had a 3.0 or above." She attended the University of Jacksonville and began working on a law degree, but switched fields and graduated in 1987 with a degree in business with a focus in advertising. "I was always very smart, hardworking and ambitious."

VII. Employment

Patient currently works as a legal secretary at Montague Sherry, a Jacksonville law firm. She plans to return to college and complete her law degree "in the next couple of years, when I've saved up some money." For additional income, she also works part-time at "Vino," a wine shop at McHenry Plaza. "I am a very good worker, and I am very focused. I am very good at my job and I plan to open my own law firm one day, like my dad. By the age of thirty, I want to be head of my own law firm." Patient has recently been experiencing dissatisfaction at work, describing her colleagues as "immature" and her job as "boring." "I really expected something more challenging. I'm bored at work and when I get home I have nothing to do either."

VIII. Social/Recreational

Patient lives alone in a rental apartment in Logan Park, though she expressed the desire to move to an apartment closer to her job. She reported that she is "pretty popular" and has "lots of friends," mostly from college. She enjoys going dancing and to nightclubs at weekends, and usually goes out with college friends, as part of a group. She is currently single after the recent breakup of a long-distance relationship. She had expected to marry this boyfriend, Martin, but "he wasn't ready." "He was really kind of immature." They are still friends, but patient feels "depressed" about the situation. She said, "I expected we would be married by now. I don't want to start dating all over again." She does not often get the opportunity to socialize because her second job means that she has to work until 9 PM most nights.

IX. Assessment / Conclusion

Begin weekly therapy to address relationship issues and situational depression.

X: Diagnosis

Axis I: 309.28 Adjustment Disorder with mixed anxiety and depressed mood.

Axis II: 301.82 Avoidant Personality Disorder.

Axis III: No diagnosis.

Axis IV: V62.89 Phase of Life Problem.

Axis V (GAF): Present functioning – 77. Highest in past year – 81.

Therapy Notes: Christina Romano, LCSW

APRIL 3: Ellen arrived ten minutes late looking anxious and depressed. We talked about the recent breakup of her 2-year long distance relationship with Martin. She said she felt "let down, depressed." She feels she'll "never meet anyone else like him." Discussed CBT, "magnifying," and "overlooking the positive." I gave her some useful positive thinking exercises to practice.

APRIL 10: Ellen arrived looking tired; greeted me with superficial smile. She told me that she feels unattractive and is worried that she is gaining weight. When I suggested the possibility of her joining a gym, she told me she is a member of The Total Gym in Riverdale but she has only been twice. We discussed techniques to avoid procrastination, including different positive thinking models. We talked about Ellen's relationship with her parents and siblings. "They'd do anything for me."

APRIL 17: Ellen arrived slightly late, looking tired. She wanted to talk about the fact she feels bored much of the time. She said, "I do not feel as though my job is challenging enough for me. I'm too smart for that job. I have too much time on my hands. That's why I started working at Vino. If I had a boyfriend, things would be different." She feels as though she started out her life with great potential, but "lost it" somewhere along the way.

APRIL 24: Appointment cancelled.

MAY 1: Ellen arrived a few minutes late, very depressed & weepy. We talked about her relationship with Martin. She misses him all the time. "Nothing of any importance ever happens in my life." "If I don't have to get up and go to work, I just sleep and sleep."

"It's so hard for me to get out of the house. I have nothing to look forward to." I tried to encourage her to keep a journal but she did not seem to be interested. "What would I write about? It would just depress me even more."

MAY 8: Ellen arrived very unhappy, tearful, miserable. We discussed antidepressants. Ellen says she has no interest in them. Has been taking St. John's Wort, recommended by her mother. Feels existential angst & misery. She feels her job is not challenging enough for her, but she has no interest in applying for other positions. Feels lonely and misunderstood, & says she spends most of her time alone, crying. Feels she is special and doesn't want to "settle" for an ordinary, dull job and boring life. Again, I tried to encourage her to keep a journal, but she said she would not find it helpful. She said she wanted to spend more time dealing with issues of her own self-esteem. We talked about her strong desire to feel less "needy and desperate," to turn this focus to other ideas and areas beyond the limited range of her work life.

MAY 15: Ellen seemed a little better today. She has spent time with her parents in Jacksonville, telling them about her problems. Says they are "understanding." More upbeat because she feels "cared for by people." Has been spending time with friends from college. We discussed emotional reasoning—where maybe we need to consider that feelings are not facts.

MAY 22: Ellen was depressed again. Very tearful, despite spending a good weekend with friends and going out on a date. St. John's Wort does not seem to be helping, she feels. Reports feeling totally overwhelmed by her problems, with no prospects at all for her future life. We discussed how Ellen could learn to put herself in a better position by making use of her intelligence, knowledge, energy, and resources to resolve the problem. I suggested she may want to try medication, but she is not interested.

MAY 29: Ellen was less weepy today, but still miserable and unhappy. We talked about the men who had asked her out—she mentioned a long list of them—but then reported faults with each one of them. Deeply wants a relationship, but admits she has impossibly high standards, and is "self-sabotaging"—very demanding and unforgiving. Again, we discussed how she feels "special," but is constantly "overlooked and ignored." I talked about "all or nothing thinking," whereas maybe Ellen can find something in between?

JUNE 5: Ellen talked about how she is so "high-strung" and easily anxious. For example, she'll convince herself she's pregnant when she knows it can't possibly be true. Manages to hold two contradictory ideas in her mind simultaneously. She talked about wanting to move out of her apartment complex into another building closer to both her jobs, but her current landlord will not let her out of the lease and she will have to continue paying rent until another tenant can be found.

JUNE 12: Ellen arrived with bruises on her face and a black eye. She said she was driving in the rain and had stopped behind another car at a red light, when the driver behind her did not stop in time and went into the back of her car, causing a pileup. She was taken to Douglas Mission Hospital for treatment for various cuts and bruises. She said she had never had an accident before and now "I think I'll be afraid to drive again." She said the accident was "a shock to my system" and "a wake-up call." We talked about over-generalization and her tendency to draw general conclusions from a single (usually negative) event, e.g. thinking that the accident is a sign that things will get worse. She seemed to comprehend the idea and said it "made sense."

JUNE 19: Did not show up. I called and left a message at her home. No response.

JUNE 22: I was visited by Officer Williams of the Clear Lake Police Department, who informed me that Ellen Watts was last seen during the early morning hours of Sunday, June 18. He reported that evidence at Ellen's apartment indicates she made it home and was interrupted. The clothes she was wearing Saturday evening were there, along with a half-eaten piece of toast, a half-smoked cigarette, and one contact lens. Her car was missing, and $900 had been removed from her bank account. A neighbor reported hearing a loud thud at approximately 04:30 on the morning of her disappearance.

No follow-up.

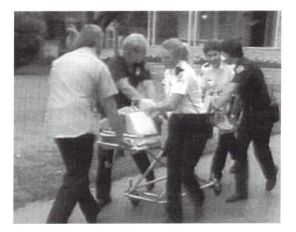

11. Audrey

Good Morning, Ladies and Gentlemen.

"Above all else, guard your heart, for it is the wellspring of life."

Today's Bible verse is from Proverbs four, twenty-three. I have a personal story I'd like to share with you with regard to this verse, and I figured the best way to do that is to just tell you about it. Last week, I called the telephone company, as we'd been having problems with static on the line. Four days later, when I was at work, a stranger knocked on the door of our home. When my wife Elizabeth opened the door, she saw a man wearing a hard yellow hat and carrying a toolbox. He had loops of cord over his shoulder and a radio clipped to his belt. When Elizabeth asked him for proof of identity, he showed her an embossed card containing his photograph, and he pointed to the phone company truck parked in front of the house. My wife was still suspicious, and she asked him to come back later when I was at home. The man said my wife could call his supervisor to confirm he was working for the company, but the truth is, Elizabeth did not trust him, and when I tell you about our past experience, perhaps you will understand why.

From what I've just told you, you might think my wife is overly suspicious, but I prefer to say that she is very careful, and she has good reason to be, because believe it or not Elizabeth and I once knew a lady who was murdered by the man who came to fix the telephone. Her name was Audrey. One day, a stranger came to Audrey's door dressed in a yellow hat and said he was from the phone company. Audrey allowed him into her house, even though she had no problem with her phone, and she had not made an appointment with the telephone company. This was a tragic mistake on her part, as it turned out this man had been stalking her for weeks, waiting for a time when her husband was not home.

It was eighteen years ago when this terrible tragedy occurred, and there is not a single day when it does not cross my mind, and I count my blessings every time. This tragedy took place when Elizabeth and I were living in a suburb of Sandridge called Eckert Hills, which was a safe, prosperous neighborhood full of churchgoing families. The lady who was murdered, Audrey Russo, lived a few blocks away from me with her husband, her little girl Amy, her son Ryan, and two dogs, Weimaraners I believe. Audrey was a homemaker and her husband was a handyman in an apartment building downtown. They were not a wealthy family but they were good Christian folks. Their front door was always open, and as I mentioned before, I believe this was a tragic mistake.

At the time our son was very young, and naturally we were anxious about leaving him during the day. Still, both Elizabeth and I had full-time responsibilities at the church, and we had no choice but to look for reliable day care. We must have looked at six or seven different facilities at least, and none of them seemed satisfactory. Either they were too expensive, or they had no organized daily schedule for the children in their care, or if they did, it was not challenging enough. For example, in one place the lady put all the children in swings or infant seats all day. A lot of them did not offer a full program of activities, or they simply showed the children videos on television for hours. Others were unnecessarily strict and rigid. For example, they did not allow parents to drop in at any time.

At that time, I was the Pastor of St. John's Methodist Church at 15th Street and Manchester in Sandridge. The Russo family also attended this church. Audrey volunteered there as well, taking care of the children. She was a calm, quiet person who never raised her voice, and she was totally devoted to the little ones. You can image how happy we were, then, one Sunday at church, when Audrey informed us she was going to start taking in children during the day. It was quite literally a gift from God. I knew she would be the perfect person to take care of Joshua, and she was.

Folks, if you know how protective Elizabeth and I are of Joshua, you will understand what kind of a person Audrey was when I say that I never had any cause to worry about our little boy when he was with her. She was a very spiritual person and a very loving, feminine woman. She once commented to me that she felt as though she had been born to be a mother. Her own little ones were so happy and well-adjusted, and they were such a good influence on Joshua.

The first time Elizabeth went over to Audrey's house in Eckert Hills, she told me that everything felt right. She said Audrey had age-appropriate toys without any of those small parts that could choke a baby or toddler. She had craft projects, collages, jigsaw puzzles, paint, and fun treats for the little ones. Sometimes she'd take the older ones on trips, such as horseback riding or the zoo. Plus, every day she had what she called "circle time," when she would focus on one letter, one color and one number. First she would show them what the letter looked like and what it sounded like, coming up with words that start with it. Then she would send them on a scavenger hunt to find something that began with that letter. It was a great way for the children to learn and be interactive, to increase retention, and I am sure any of you with children of your own know how important this is. She would incorporate those kinds of activities into circle time every day. However, she also saved time for free play, allowing each child to play as they wished, as well as active play, when all the children would play together. They would play tag outside, or kick a ball around, or just good old fashioned hide and seek. Any way for them to expend lots of energy before heading home.

Well as you can imagine, folks, our little boy always had a great time at Audrey's house. Often, when Elizabeth would arrive to pick him up after work, he would be playing with Ryan or one of the other little boys and he would not want to go home. So she would simply pull up a chair and Audrey would get her some coffee and a homemade muffin, and they would chat, often for an hour or more. That is just the way Audrey was, friendly and relaxed. She always had time to sit and chat. She was a real people person. Steve, her husband, was the same way.

I should also mention that Audrey was a gifted piano player. Sometimes when Elizabeth went by to pick up our son, she would hear her playing for the children. Folks, it pains me to tell you this, but it is believed that the man who killed her heard her playing the piano, and he became obsessed and started to spy on her and stalk her. He would walk by her house and listen to her play. They said he had been spying on her for weeks. Since he did not know her name, he referred to her privately as "The Piano Lady." He drove over to her house one morning, close to lunchtime, dressed as a telephone repairman, and she let him in.

Folks, Audrey was strangled with a nylon stocking, and stabbed. They took her to Eckert Hills Hospital, but it was too late, she had already passed on.

Now, you may be wondering why I am telling you all this. It has to do with today's verse, from Proverbs four, twenty-three: "Above all else, guard your heart, for it is the wellspring of life." I'm telling you this story in order to help you understand how I have come to be so careful in my life. This tragic incident made such an impression on Elizabeth and myself that it would not be saying too much to say that it changed our life. Most of all, it taught us that nobody is above suspicion.

You see, folks, Audrey Russo's murderer was a college educated, family man. Believe it or not, he was the president of his church and leader of a Boy Scout troop. He went to church every Sunday for thirty years, and he murdered at least ten women. What that tells me is there is nobody you can trust.

Let me tell you folks about this man. Ironically, he worked for a home security company for many years, though he was fired when all his coworkers complained that he was arrogant and confrontational.

Next he became a compliance supervisor of animal control, nuisances, cars left in the street and so forth. After that, he was appointed to the Eckert County Animal Control Advisory Board on the recommendation of the county commissioner, and when he resigned, guess what? The mayor presented him with an award for ten years of service.

Folks, I believe this man gravitated to these positions of responsibility because he was addicted to the sin of power, and liked to impose his power on other people, particularly women. For example, one of his neighbors once saw him measuring another neighbor's lawn with a ruler, and then he called the city to complain that the grass was too long. He often said he worked for the police department, but in fact he did not. His job allowed him to get access to women's homes. He even rigged one lady's alarm so he could get back into her house. A number of women complained about harassment, but they were told the man was only doing his job.

I have never forgotten what happened to Audrey Russo, may her soul rest in peace. I hope you will now understand why I am so careful. And I would encourage you, especially you ladies, always to stay alert to your surroundings, try not to go out alone after dark, do not let your guard down when a stranger smiles or greets you, and never, ever, ever let a stranger into your home when your husband is away. As we learn in Psalm one hundred and eighteen, verse eight:

"It is better to trust in the Lord than to put confidence in man."

Let us Pray.

12. Vicky

<u>Sunday September 6, 1970</u>:
Breakfast: 1 bowl oatmeal with blueberries, no sugar, black coffee.
Lunch: 1 tuna sandwich with mayo.
Dinner: baked potato, cheese, slice of peach and apricot pie.
Snacks: 1 apple, 3 oatmeal cookies.
Drinks: 2 vodka martinis.

This new girl Vicky was on my shift last night. I told her that most of the issues we deal with are secondary, there's not much here in the way of critical care. Two drunks in the casino and one psycho who needed a MASSIVE dose of Haldol. I squirted myself in the face with the arterial line I was setting up and it took us ten minutes before we could stop laughing. Vicky wants to lose 15–20 pounds, so she's going to join me on my diet. That will be so cool. She told me about a school friend of hers from North Carolina who has celiac disease and can only eat gluten-free foods, which she says are much better for you than wheat. They don't spike your levels so you feel full longer. I told her, eating a healthy diet isn't easy when you work in a casino.

This is her first time working a night shift, so I gave her some tips.

At first, I remember, my body didn't want to sleep when the sun was shining. That's just how bodies are. I explained to Vicky how I walk round the lake after work and get everything done round the house in the morning, so I can lie down and relax and learn to sleep during the day.

Vicky gave me some great diet advice. She's moving into Marengo Village tomorrow, so we'll be neighbors. I told her to get dark colored drapes so the daylight won't come through, and to take the phone out of the wall and set her alarm clock for about an hour before she needs to be at work, enough time to eat and take a shower.

I love my job, I love my team. There are so many great people here. Going into nursing was the best decision I ever made. I love being on top of my game at all times. Every day is something different.

Monday September 7, 1970:
Breakfast: 2 poached eggs, 1 slice of wheat toast.
Lunch: ham and avocado salad with tomato dressing.
Dinner: pasta with tomato sauce, handful of potato chips, 4oz baked beans.
Snacks: pb&j; sunflower seeds.
Drinks: black coffee no sugar.

Came home and packed my work bag and an extra set of scrubs, then I had some tea and a long bubble bath with candles before I went to sleep. This morning Vicky did not show up for work. She signed out of the nurse's station last night two hours after I left, at midnight. Culler sent me to knock on the door to her new condo, but there was no answer. Rachel told me she saw Vicky late last night walking past her apartment with a blonde man. Her car was still at Los Robles. We looked at the logbook. She signed out at 1:50 AM and left her uniform at the nurse's station. Her handwriting looks weird in the book, kind of shaky. Nobody saw her leaving the casino. Cullen called the cops and Mrs. Lloyd let us into Vicky's apartment and (thank god) she wasn't lying there, but there was no sign of her. All that's missing are her clothes and her purse. Nobody has a clue. Everybody is terrified. It's so creepy!

This evening a guy was walking in the parking lot with a mug of hot chocolate and this other guy came over and slapped him on the back, and the first guy just threw the hot chocolate over his shoulder right into the other guy's face. First-degree burns. We had to make him lie down and cover his face with ice packs till the pain went away. He was talking about suing the casino for damages. I told him good luck with that one.

Tuesday September 8, 1970:
Breakfast: farina, 1 boiled egg, milk.
Lunch: 4 fish sticks, baked beans, tomato sauce.
Dinner: Chinese stir-fried rice, slice of custard pie.
Snacks: 1 banana, 4 cookies.
Drinks: 2 vodka martinis.

Got home and took a hot bath with Epsom salts, packed my lunch bag ready to go and my work bag and my hoodie jacket. Vicky has still not shown up and the cops came to interview us. They wanted us to remember everything we could that she said about her friends, especially boyfriends. This cop from the South Lake police department interviewed me. He asked me to tell him everything I knew about Vicky. There wasn't too much that could help him. I said she told me she grew up on a farm in North Carolina, she had a lot of brothers and sisters, maybe eight or nine. She was a member of Future Homemakers of America. I know after she finished nursing school she lived in Florida and she worked at a hospital in Boca Raton, and quit when she got a job as a private travel nurse for some rich doctor and went on a lot of trips with him in his private plane. He asked me why she quit that job and I said I didn't know. Maybe the guy died? He asked me to describe her and I said she was about five-four, one hundred and thirty-nine pounds (I knew that exactly because she told me her target weight was one-twenty), brown hair with blonde frosted hi-lites, blue eyes. Oh, and she wore contacts. He said that was very good info, nobody else had told him that.

So then after the cops had gone Terri got pulled into Cullen's office, he was yelling at her. She said he accused her of "providing consistently unsafe patient care." That's just crazy talk. None of her patients have ever complained about her. Cullen's held it against her ever since she dumped him. Now he's going to put all her charts under review. He also accused her of breaking patient confidentiality by talking to me about the drunk who came in last night. Insane! Cullen is just freaking out about Vicky. We all are!!

<u>Wednesday September 9, 1970:</u>
Breakfast: omelet, oatmeal, milk, grapefruit juice.
Lunch: pb&j on wheat bread.
Dinner: baked tilapia, potato wedges with bbq seasoning, half a strawberry light couscous cake.
Snack: 6 saltines, 2 oranges, 1 banana, carrots with ranch dip.

Fruit is good for snacks because it has natural sugars that give you energy. Got home and took a bath with Johnson and Johnson's Lavender Baby Bath to help me relax. Ironed my scrubs. Feel as though my body is in gear to the night shift rhythm now, and it's becoming natural for me. I don't have many problems relaxing any more, now I have all my tips and snacks.

Terri told me that Cullen and Mrs. Lloyd both got creepy calls from this guy who said he was a friend of Vicky's and that she was sick and had to go home because of a family emergency, and that she wouldn't be moving into her apartment after all. Everybody thinks it sounds weird. The cops think it's a hoax and she's been kidnapped, maybe by somebody who was in the casino and saw her and followed her home. How did this guy know the numbers to call? Did Vicky give them to him? It's been on the local news and in all the papers. Everybody is freaking out! Some people think she picked up some guy in the casino but I just can't imagine her doing something like that. But then, I didn't know her that well. I just met her, actually. When the cop asked me about her boyfriends I told him she didn't have any. But what do I know? They asked me if there was anybody at the casino I didn't trust, and I told them I never trust the security guards because they're so underpaid, they'll do anything for extra money, and I don't blame them, they get no training at all, except every so often we'll get a retired cop.

Busy night after the holiday weekend; five drunks, some guy on drugs, and an old man fell in the bathroom and broke his leg. No stabbings or suicides, though. I know I'm lucky to work here, and it's pretty well staffed, but tonight was real bad, Terri was off sick with a cold and I had to work without a break and stay overtime. At one point I was feeling so overwhelmed and stressed-out, I had to go outside for a moment and take a few deep breaths and get my thoughts together and try to relax. By the time my shift was over all I wanted to do was to crawl under the covers and pass out, but I couldn't sleep all day and my neck hurt and I couldn't stop thinking about Vicky. Made sure to double lock the front door!!

<u>Thursday September 10, 1970</u>:
Breakfast: oatmeal, blueberries, no sugar, black coffee.
Lunch: tuna salad sandwich.
Dinner: chicken breast, French fries, corn, cottage cheese, lite rice pudding.
Snacks: 4 chocolates, 1 apple.
Drinks: 3 vodka martinis.

They've brought in this new girl, Debra, to replace Vicky. She used to work in pediatric hematology oncology. I gave her all the same tips I gave Vicky, about how to change over her circadian rhythms to stay awake and alert at night. I told her it's hard at first, and you have to stick to the same sleep cycle at weekends even when you're not working, otherwise it's no good. You've got to be disciplined.

Still no news about Vicky. Some people have been saying maybe she just left with a guy she met in the casino. She had a new car and new condo and lots of new clothes. Plus, what about the guy who made the phone call? The cops have been searching the woods. It's terrible. They're talking about dredging the lake. I think someone saw her at the casino and got fixated on her and waited for her to finish her shift. I remember that girl who used to work the night shift, Margaret, who was attracting stalkers left and right. She had to be escorted home every night. What if the guy who took Vicky was waiting there for her when I left? It's almost too scary to think about. Talked to Vicky's mom on the phone. She was frantic.

Single shift. Must be a full moon because we had psychos all night. Middle-aged drunk lady complaining of palpitations and diaphoresis. I ask her to tell me what she's taken and she tells me that she thinks some guy spiked her drinks. Yeah, right, lady. Then this guy came into the casino stark naked! The security guys turned him out and called the cops, and they said they'd get to it when they had time. Typical cops. Me and Debra watched through the window and he was out there for like thirty minutes with police cars driving by. None of them bothered to stop. Go figure. Like I told Debra, it's a pretty interesting job. We encounter some very interesting characters.

Friday September 11, 1970:
Breakfast: banana yogurt with granola.
Lunch: 1 large mushroom stuffed with cheese and garlic.
Dinner: 1 burrito, rice, beans, menudo, salad.
Snacks: 1 piece of wheat toast with nutella, 8 saltines.
Drinks: 1 beer.

Debra told me she read that people who work the night shift have an increased chance of getting certain kinds of cancer. It had something to do with melatonin. But somebody has to work the night shift, and there are lots of other people doing it here so it's never lonely. There are croupiers and bartenders and security guards. There's no real nighttime in a casino. And now I've got enough self-care skills to keep healthy. I eat well and watch what I eat and walk round the lake practically every other day and I try to be consistent. I still want to lose fifteen pounds though.

Terri was on the radio talking about Vicky. She said, "Everybody's on eggshells and stressed-out and we just want the police to tell us what's going on." She said she has not slept since Vicky went missing. The cops have been leaving flyers under car windscreen wipers in the parking lot and searching people's back yards in town.

Late shift. This fifty-something-year-old man lost his family's life savings in the casino and tried to kill himself with an overdose of benzos. He asks me to bring him a Bible because he wants to repent to God for gambling and trying to kill himself. I asked around but there didn't seem to be a single Bible in the entire casino. Felt real sorry for the guy.

Saturday September 12, 1970:
Breakfast: egg-white omelet with spinach.
Lunch: onion bagel with lox, capers and cream cheese.
Dinner: small chicken breast, hashbrowns.
Snacks: 1 Baby Ruth, 1 banana.
Drinks: 1 beer.

The cops have been searching the mountains with helicopters and on the radio they said the FBI were getting involved. Terri wants to have a candlelight vigil. A neat idea, I think. The cops say they've been given a lot of tips and some good leads. I only hope the person who kidnapped her is keeping her safe nearby. Her mom has come up from North Carolina. "My heart knows she's alive," she said on the radio, "but I feel we're running out of time." The cop on the radio said it's important that she took her purse with her. She has money and ID, so at least, it's a good sign. He said, "the worst-scenario criminal investigation will involve a sexual kidnapping or predatory behavior. We're not looking at that right now." Thank god. Some people wanted to hand out flyers in the casino but Cullen says it would be bad for business. He said people don't want to think about missing girls when they're having fun and spending money, and I guess he's right.

Quiet night. I only had three patients. I took a two-hour nap. Bliss! An old lady came in with dental pain. She had stinking breath and when she opened her mouth, two of her molars were missing and the place where they'd been was just a void filled with yellow pus. She said her teeth fell out "just a few hours ago" and she'd tried to cure herself with prayer and crystals. Crystal meth, more like. I had to clean out her mouth. She told me I was a "sweetie pie." She was definitely on something. Still, for the most part, as I said to Debra, people who come here are pretty much decent people, just like anywhere else in America.

<u>Sunday September 13, 1970</u>:
Breakfast: yogurt with granola.
Lunch: baked beans and whole wheat toast.
Dinner: pizza with cheese and artichoke hearts.
Snacks: handful of potato chips, 1 orange, 2 graham crackers. Raisins for a pick-me-up.
Drinks: 2 beers.

Got home late and drank hot tea in the bath. Terri asked me to work New Year's Eve and I said I'd get back to her but I guess I will. It's good money and it can be a lot of fun as long as there's not too many crazy drunks. Was planning to get up early and kick-start my body with a power shower but instead I stayed in bed, talked on the phone to Mom. She told me Jeannie is retiring at last, thank god. That woman is nosy and inappropriate. She's in her 60s and one time my mom said she drove past our house just to see how big it was. Mom said she just sits at her desk and will not move for anyone the whole eight hours she is working. Talking to Mom makes me realize how lucky I am in my job and the people I work with. I've never felt so welcomed, stimulated or encouraged. I realize that having a job like this is a miracle and I'll never take it for granted and do just the bare minimum to get by like some people do. We have a good team and some of the people here are phenomenal. Okay, there's always a little drama and it's not always pretty, but most of the time everybody puts aside their differences and we all get along together.

Terri came over and we went out for pizza and beer. We've sure earned it!

13. Mirasol

I dreamed I was on the sampan in Balayan Bay. I was lying on my back, watching the sun as it moved in and out of the clouds. The oars were locked. I could hear my father humming as he cast his nets, the water lapping the side of the boat. Up on the hill, the bells of St. Francisco's began to ring. Five o'clock. It was the alarm. I opened my eyes and tried to move, but my wrists were tied behind my back. I could not feel my arms. Then I remembered.

It happened on the eighteenth of August, 1967. I was 24 years old. There were not enough dormitories for all the nurses, so they put some of us in houses not far from the hospital. Our house backed on to a park. That was the way the man came in, through the park at night. He pulled the screen out of the kitchen window, then reached round and unlocked the back door.

There were eight of us living there: Dalisay, Amihan, myself, Mirasol, and five American girls. The Americans were kind and friendly to us, but I am sad to say we did not mix with them. We were shy and talked in our own language. The director of nursing,

Mrs. Doon, was also a Filipino, and the American girls thought we were Mrs. Doon's spies. Needless to say, this was not true.

We had arrived only ten weeks earlier, and were struggling with our English, our classes, and our new way of life. Of course, we thought America was fine, dizzy, exciting and wonderful. The other girls seemed very sophisticated to us. In the evenings, they would go to clubs and bars, or stay out on dates. Yet they were still students, while we were trained nurses, on a salary. Dalisay sent more than half her money back home. She came from Jones City, a hundred and fifty miles north of Manila, and her family was very poor. But she had a promising future. She had two admirers at home that she wrote to—a doctor and a dentist. We joked with her about which one she was going to choose. She sent the dentist a record by Jerry Vale, *There Goes My Heart*. Amihan and I made fun of her.

That will be my first and last gift to him, she said to us.

The hospital Jeep picked us up every morning at six-thirty, and if we were late, we had to walk. We started work at seven and finished at three-thirty, when the Jeep would bring us home. Then the three of us would go to Foodland to buy rice, fish, tomatoes, pineapple and spices. We made what we knew: *cocidos, torta*, *kare-kare*. We had bought our own pots, pans, and glasses out of our wages, because I am sorry to say the American girls were not clean. Dishes were supposed to be washed and dried within an hour of the meal, but if the American girls cooked, they often left dishes in the sink. Happily, they did not use the kitchen often. Mostly, they ate take-away food.

That day, when Amihan and I got back from the hospital, Dalisay was already in the kitchen, making *pancit*. We ate together, then, after washing the dishes, we went upstairs for a short nap. When we woke, around six, Amihan and Dalisay watched television and wrote letters home, while I washed my uniform by hand in the upstairs bathroom. If our uniforms were not clean, we would earn demerits from Mrs. Doon.

Dalisay went to bed at ten-fifteen, and at ten-thirty I locked the door and followed her upstairs. I was about to turn off the light, when Amihan asked me to wait a moment. She wanted to say her prayers. She knelt down by her bed in her white pajamas while I climbed into the top bunk and drifted off to sleep.

That night, I did not say my prayers.

Why? I do not know.

Perhaps I was not ready to die.

We were woken by four knocks on the bedroom door. The light was still on. I looked at the clock. It was just after eleven. I got down from my bunk, unlocked the door and opened it a little. He pushed me inside, a tall man dressed in black, with a pockmarked face and a gun in his hand. Amihan was sitting up in bed, staring at us.

Where are your friends? said the man, grabbing my arm. Come on. Show me where they are. You too.

We led him to the large bedroom and he made us go through the door ahead of him. He did not turn on the light. Dalisay was awake, and when she saw the man, she jumped out of bed and ran into the closet. I ran after her, and so did Amihan. We slammed the door closed. I grabbed the handle and held it tight. Inside, the three of us hid in the dark among nursing uniforms, party dresses, cloaks and hats. We took each other's hands and prayed. We could not hear what was happening because there were two fans on in the room.

After a while someone turned off the fans and knocked on the door.

It was the girl called Karen.

He wants you to come out, she said. He's not going to hurt us. He just wants money.

She did not seem afraid.

When we came out, the lights were on. The American girls were sitting in a row with their backs against the dressers. The girl with the short dark hair had come in from her bedroom. The man had his left arm around the waist of the big girl, and he told us to sit down. We were all in a line underneath the back windows that overlooked the park. Then he told the big girl to sit down as well, and he turned off the light. There was a small gap between the bedroom curtains.

The man sat down with us on the floor, stretched out his legs, and started talking. He kept very close to the big girl. She was his favorite, I believe. I could not understand much of what he said. His voice was very soft. He had short hair and his ears stuck out. I looked at his face very closely. And even though he had many pockmarks, I thought he was handsome, in a way.

Before long, we got used to the dark. The light from the park allowed us to see one another. At that time, I thought he wanted money, nothing more. And I knew two of the girls were not there. I thought perhaps they had gone for help.

The man smoked a cigarette. He talked to us and his voice was always gentle.

How did you get in? asked Karen.

Through the door, the man smiled.

She laughed.

He went on talking softly.

I understood enough to know that he wanted to go to Memphis. I recognized the name of the city even though I had never heard it spoken. I had only read it in books and magazines.

Then he pointed his gun at each of us in turn, and asked us how much money we had. The American girls had small amounts—two dollars, four dollars, five dollars. Dalisay, Amihan and I had more. I had ten dollars.

Where is your money? he asked Karen.

In my purse. There, on my bed. She pointed to her bunk.

Get it for me, said the man.

She got up, took the money from her purse and gave it to him. He was pointing his gun at her all the time. When she gave him the money, he moved the gun to his left hand and put the bills in his pocket.

Next, he said.

One by one, we gave him whatever money we had.

There was not a great deal of money, all in all. I wondered if there was enough for him to get to Memphis. I did not know how far Memphis was.

Then we all heard the back door slam, and we heard Marcie's voice. She was calling Mrs. Doon next door, to check in.

The man looked nervous. He stood and walked up and down, with his gun in his hand. Then we heard Marcie running upstairs, singing to herself. The man went to the door, held the handle, and, when Marcie got close, he pulled the door open. She gave a little cry of surprise. He pointed his gun at her and told her to sit down with the rest of us.

Do you have any money? he asked her.

Sure, she said, opening her purse and taking out her wallet.

Give it here, he said.

Do you want coins, too?

No, just bills.

Are you sure? You may need to make a phone call.

She did not fear the man. She spoke to him like a friend.

He put the gun on a bunk, pulled a sheet off one of the beds, stepped on the end of it, took a knife from his belt and started tearing the sheet into thin strips. He hung each strip around his neck as he tore the next. I could see the flash of his knife in the moonlight. It looked like the knife my father used to gut fish. The blade was three inches long.

He tied up the big girl first. He tied a strip of sheet round one of her ankles, knotted it, then looped the ends round her other ankle and tied them together. Very gently, he asked her to turn over face down on the floor. He told her to put her hands behind her back, palms upward, and tied her wrists together with a double loop. He told her to turn around, sit up and face him. She struggled. He had to help her up.

After the big girl, he slid over and tied Marcie in the same way.

You don't have to tie me up, she told him. I'll do anything you want.

She did not sound frightened. She sounded brave. She made me feel strong.

Just do what I tell you, said the man.

When he had finished, he told her to turn over. She began to struggle, so he scooped her up and put her on a bottom bunk, face up. I thought he was going to rape her then, because he had laid her on the bed, but he did not.

He tied Dalisay and the girl with the dark hair in the same way, talking to them in a soft voice, telling them everything was all right, he was not going to hurt them. When he was tying me, his body felt large and hot. He smelled of alcohol, on his sweat and his skin, as well as his breath. Whenever I smell alcohol now, I remember this man.

Then we were all tied up.

Pointing his gun at us one by one, he counted.

One, two, three, four, five, six, seven.

The man stretched, looked out of the window, then went back to the big girl and, taking his knife, cut the strips of sheet binding her ankles.

Stand up, he told her.

She was wearing blue-and-white short pajamas. He took her arm.

Come on, he said. Come with me.

She spat in his face.

Hey, said the man.

He took a sheet and wiped his face with it. Then he pulled her out of the room. He left the door open, but a crack of light was all we could see.

I was sitting up with my wrists tied behind my back. I looked around the room. In front of me, there were four brassieres hanging off the bed frame to dry. On the chest of drawers, there was a Bible, nursing books, a teddy bear, framed photographs, an empty champagne bottle, and four cans of hair spray. We had to wear our hair in a manner that promoted safety and professionalism. It had to be above the collar and off the face.

We must call for help, I whispered.

No, the girl with dark hair whispered back.

Nobody will hear us, anyway, said Karen. The girls next door are on vacation.

She was correct. Still, I wanted to fight. I did not want to lie still, tied up, waiting to be raped.

The man had turned off the fans and it was very hot. When I craned my neck I could see the clock on the dresser, but I could not see the time.

Then, from the hallway, we heard the big girl make a noise like Ah!

We must fight him, I whispered again. The next person he unties must scream. They must throw the lamp through the window.

No, whispered the dark-haired girl. We should treat him like a patient in the emergency room. We must keep quiet and calm.

Then we heard voices outside, the back door opening and closing, and footsteps and laughing on the stairs. The girl called Anne had come home with a friend. They ran upstairs and went straight into Anne's room, and there he was. Through the crack in the door, I saw the man's figure blocking off the stairs. Then Anne and her friend ran into our room and stared at us all, sitting tied up on the floor. They started to laugh. They did not understand what was happening. They were both wearing Bermuda shorts.

The man followed them.

You two, come here now, he said.

They stood there, frozen.

Come here, he said, louder. Then he came over and grabbed Anne's arm and led them both out of the room.

I do not know what happened next. I turned my head away and tried to not to see. There was a cry, then a door banged shut and I could hear nothing else. Amihan's eyes were shining with fear, but Marcie had fallen asleep. I do not think she knew what was happening. Even though I do not approve of drinking, I confess that I envied her.

The man was away for a long time. After a while, we heard water running in the bathroom and we heard the toilet flush. Then he came back into the room with his knife, glanced out of the window, then went straight over to the girl with dark hair and cut the sheets binding her ankles. She was wearing a long nightdress, brightly colored and see-through. The man took her out of the room. Again, he did not close the door all the way. Again, we heard the Ah! sound.

After that, we all started rolling and flapping across the floor, like fish. We all rolled to different corners of the room. I rolled from side to side then forward on my stomach. I hid under Dalisay's bunk, but I could not get my head all the way in.

Again I heard the sound of running water in the tub. For a moment I thought he was going to take a bath. I did not know he was washing the blood away.

My two friends were pressed against the wall on the other side of the room.

The man came back, looked out of the window again, and went over to them. He chose Dalisay. She was the smallest, even smaller than me, and I am only four feet ten. He did not untie her. He simply scooped her up and carried her out. We were all very small compared to the Americans. We noticed it every day at the hospital. Some of the patients were as big as water buffalo.

Soon I heard Dalisay say Ah! like the others, but she was closer, and it was louder. Then the water came again. Then he came back into the room for Amihan, my best friend. This was very hard for me. I was weeping and I pressed my forehead to the floor. I heard him lift up Amihan and carry her out. The last thing I saw was a glimpse of her white shorts. Then I heard her cry *Masakit*! which, in our language, means It hurts! Then she made the same Ah! noise that the others had made.

I never saw my best friend again.

Now only three of us were left. Karen and myself were on the floor, and Marcie was asleep on the bunk. When he came back, I still had not got my head out of view and I was afraid he would see me. I pressed my knees against the floor. Karen tried to hide, too, but she was not small like me.

She was whimpering in pain. The man came over to her.

Will you please untie my ankles first?

He untied her ankles.

Then, in his soft voice, he said, Are you the girl in the yellow dress?

She did not reply. I wondered if she knew him. Perhaps he had seen her before, in the park.

He led her outside—to the bathroom this time. I could tell because of the echo.

Lie down here, I heard him say.

Lie down here! he repeated, in a louder voice.

After a long time, I heard water running again.

I pushed myself tightly against the wall, lay completely still, and waited. It was very dusty under the bed. Right in front of my eyes was a small piece of dried stool from Marcie's kitten. She was not supposed to have the kitten. Pets were not allowed. Mrs. Doon made her give it to the Animal Society. It was not hygienic, she said, and I agreed.

I could hear Marcie breathing deeply, tied up in her bunk. Then I heard the man coming back into the room. I closed my eyes and tried to pray.

He slammed the bedroom door shut with a bang. Marcie woke up at once.

She said, I dreamed that my mother died.

I heard him cutting her bonds with his knife. Then I heard him sit down on the bed. He unzipped her jeans and pulled them off, along with her panties. Then I heard him climb on top of her.

Have you done this before?

Marcie did not reply. After a while the springs started to squeak and groan. Then I heard him say, politely, Would you mind putting your legs around my back?

After the man had finished, he went to open the bedroom door, then came back, lifted Marcie up and carried her out. I saw them leave the room. I closed my eyes again. I could hear him carrying her downstairs.

That is when I decided to move. I knew I had to be fast. I did not know when the man would be back. I squeezed out of my hiding place, rolled on my front across the floor, and struggled under the opposite bunk. I knew there would be enough room to hide myself, and the sheets and blankets were hanging down off the bed at both sides. I thought perhaps the man would not see me there.

I lay waiting for him to come back, and after a long time, he did. He turned on the light. There was a small gap between two sheets, and I could see him looking round the room. He took a purse, shook it, and a bill fluttered to the ground. He bent over to pick it up. He was right in front of me. I could smell him. I closed my eyes.

I did not breathe for a long time. The house was silent, but I had not heard the front door close. I thought he was still in the house. I did not know, then, that he had walked off into the night, leaving the door wide open.

The alarm clock stopped ringing, and everything was silent. Though it was still dark, I could feel the sun beginning to rise. I rolled from side to side on my stomach, hauling myself out from under the bunk, and then rubbing myself against the bed frame. Once I was sitting up, I could make fists and move my arms around behind my back until I felt the bonds begin to grow loose, and then I wriggled my thumbs free and pulled my wrists out of the knots.

Suddenly, the second alarm went off. I was very frightened, because I thought the man was still downstairs. I waited until the noise had stopped, then I looked out of the bedroom door and saw legs and blood. I ran into my bedroom. There were three dead girls on the floor, and the carpet was black and sticky. I climbed up to the top of my bunk by the window and pushed out the screen. Then I climbed on the ledge overhanging the front door and started to cry. I wanted to scream for help, but—I don't know why—I could only weep.

After a few minutes, a girl came out.

They are all dead, I told her. Everybody on the sampan is dead.

I do not remember saying it, but that is what I said.

The girl was in her nightdress. She was looking up at me. She went back and got her robe and slippers, then returned. I could tell she was about to go in the house, and I tried to stop her. I jumped down off the ledge, ten feet they said. But it was too late. The girl was running out of the house. Someone led me next door and told me to lie down. Not too long after that, the police came, with a doctor who gave me an injection that put me to sleep.

I saw the man twice more after that. The first time was in the hospital after he had tried to take his own life. They were sure it was him. I put on my uniform and followed the sister on her morning rounds. When we got to his bed, I was afraid of him. I thought he would recognize me, but he did not. He was half asleep. I stared at him for a long time, his pockmarks, his blue eyes and sticking-out ears. He smiled at me.

Yes, it was really him.

I saw him once again, the following year, in the witness box.

I was not afraid of him then.

Appendix

1. Lisa

In the early morning of Sunday, July 31, 1977, Stacy Moskowitz and Bobby Violante, parked in a quiet spot near Gravesend Bay, were shot through the car windscreen by David Berkowitz, better known as the "Son of Sam." Violante was almost blinded, but survived. Stacy Moskowitz died thirty-eight hours after the shooting. Berkowitz was convicted of killing six people and wounding several others in the course of eight shootings in New York between 1976 and 1977. He is currently serving a life sentence in Sullivan Correctional Facility in Fallsburg, New York.

Works Consulted

George Carpozi Jr., *Son of Sam: The .44 Caliber Killer*, New York, Manor Books, 1977.

Maury Terry, *The Ultimate Evil*, New York, Doubleday & Co., 1987.

2. Tracy

On January 12, 1975, 23-year-old Caryn Campbell left her physician boyfriend in the lobby of the Wildwood Inn in Apsen, Colorado, to get a magazine from the couple's room. She was seen walking down the second floor hallway toward the room, but she never returned. On February 18, Campbell's nude body was found in a snowbank 25 feet off the road. She had died of repeated blunt instrument blows to her skull, and also suffered deep cuts from a sharp weapon. In January 1989, days before his execution, serial killer Ted Bundy confessed to the crime.

WORKS CONSULTED

Anne Rule, *The Stranger Beside Me*, New York, Signet, 1981.

Stephen G. Michaud and Hugh Aynesworth, *The Only Living Witness*, New York, Signet, 1989.

3. Cheryl

Geralyn DeSoto was found stabbed to death in her trailer home in Addis, Louisiana on January 14, 2002. Although her husband was the primary suspect, DNA evidence revealed that her assailant was the Baton Rouge Serial Killer, Derrick Todd Lee, who is believed to have been responsible for the deaths of seven women in the Baton Rouge and Lafayette areas. Lee is currently on death row at the Louisiana State Penitentiary.

WORKS CONSULTED

Susan D. Mustafa, Tony Clayton and Sue Israel, *Blood Bath*, St. Louis, LA, Pinnacle Press, 2009.

Susan D. Mustafa, *I've Been Watching You: The South Louisiana Serial Killer*, Bloomington, IN, AuthorHouse, 2006.

4. Valerie

On Wednesday, May 8, 1963, Beverly Samans, a 23-year-old graduate student, was found murdered in her Boston apartment. She is widely believed to be the tenth victim of Albert DeSalvo, the Boston Strangler. Police speculated that because of her singing she had developed very strong throat muscles that may have made strangulation more difficult and resulted in her stabbing. DeSalvo was stabbed to death in prison in 1973.

WORKS CONSULTED

Susan Kelly, *The Boston Stranglers*, New York, Diane Publishing Company, 1995.

Casey Sherman and Dick Lehr, *A Rose for Mary: The Hunt for the Real Boston Strangler*, Boston, MA, Northeastern University Press, 2003.

5. Nancy

On Wednesday, April 1, 1998, the badly decomposed body of thirty-four-year-old Linda Maybin was found in the 4800 block of East Fourteenth Avenue in Spokane, Washington. Maybin had been working as a prostitute and was known to use illicit drugs, particularly crack cocaine. She had been missing for five months. In April 2000, Robert Lee Yates, 48, was charged with eight counts of first-degree murder in the deaths of Spokane area prostitutes, and was suspected in the deaths of as many as 18 women, including Linda Maybin. Yates is currently on death row at the Washington State Penitentiary.

WORKS CONSULTED

Burl Barer, *Body Count*, St. Louis, LA, Pinnacle Press, 2002.

Mark Fuhrman, *Murder in Spokane*, New York, Avon Books, 2002.

6. Alice

On November 23, 1977, the badly decomposed body of Jane King, 28, an actress and former Scientologist, was found near an off-ramp of the Golden State Freeway. King was found to be a victim of the Hillside Strangler, the media sobriquet given to two cousins, Kenneth Bianchi and Angelo Buono, who were convicted of kidnapping, raping, torturing, and killing girls ranging in age from 12 to 28 during a four-month period from late 1977 through early 1978. Bianchi is serving a life sentence in the Washington State Penitentiary of the Washington State Department of Corrections in Walla Walla, Washington. Buono died of a heart attack on September 21, 2002, in Calipatria State Prison of the California Department of Corrections, where he was serving a life sentence.

WORKS CONSULTED

Darcy O'Brien, *The Hillside Stranglers*, New York, Running Press, 2003.

Ted Schwartz, *The Hillside Strangler: A Murderer's Mind*, New York, Signet, 1982.

7. Louise

On the morning of April 27, 1991, a transient in Riverside County, California, stumbled upon the body of 24-year-old Cherie Michelle Payseur, a part-time maid who also worked as a prostitute. She had been raped and strangled, and her body, penetrated by a toilet plunger, was left in a bowling alley parking lot. In July 1995, a jury found William Lee Suff guilty of killing twelve women, including Cherie Payseur, though police suspect he may be responsible for as many as 22 deaths. Suff is currently on death row at San Quentin Prison.

WORKS CONSULTED

Brian Lane and Bill Suff, *Cat and Mouse: Mind Games with a Serial Killer*, New York, Dove Books, 1997.

Christine Keers and Dennis St. Pierre, *The Riverside Killer*, Pinnacle Press, St. Louis, MO, 1996.

8. Kayla

Tiffany Bresciani worked as a prostitute to support her drug habit and that of her boyfriend Dave Rubinstein, cofounder of the New York punk band Reagan Youth. On June 24, 1993, Bresciani was picked up by a regular customer, and told Rubinstein she would return in twenty minutes. She never came back. A few days later, two New York state troopers pulled over a truck on Long Island's Southern State Parkway and found Bresciani's body in the back. The driver, Joel Rifkin, was later linked to the murders of numerous prostitutes. Rifkin was found guilty of nine counts of second-degree murder in 1994 and sentenced to 203 years to life. He is currently housed in the Clinton Correctional Facility in Clinton County, New York. Dave Rubinstein committed suicide two weeks after Tiffany's body was discovered.

WORKS CONSULTED

Robert Mladinich, *From the Mouth of the Monster: The Joel Rifkin Story*, New York, Pocket Books, 2001.

Maria Eftimiades, *Garden of Graves, The Shocking True Story of Long Island Serial Killer Joel Rifkin*, New York, St. Martin's Press, 1993.

9. Emi

On the night of September 14, 1972, Edmund Kemper, the Co-Ed Killer, abducted a 15-year-old hitchhiker, Aiko Koo. While keeping her at gunpoint, Kemper stopped his car at the side of a road and strangled Koo to death with her scarf. He placed her body in the trunk of his car and drove back to his mother's house, where he raped and dismembered the body. He later buried the remains in his mother's backyard. At his trial, Kemper pleaded insanity, but he was found guilty of eight counts of murder. He asked for the death penalty, but received life imprisonment. Kemper remains among the general prison population at California Medical Facility in Vacaville, California.

WORKS CONSULTED

Margaret Cheney, *The Co-Ed Killer*, New York, Walker & Co., 1976.

Ward Damio, *Urge to Kill*, New York, Pinnacle Books, 1974.

10. Ellen

Joan Butler was last seen during the early morning hours of Sunday, June 18, 1989, when she left her friends to return home to her apartment in Kansas City. Evidence indicates she made it home, but her car was missing, and cash had been removed from her bank account. A neighbor reported hearing a loud thud at approximately 04:30 on the morning of her disappearance. Richard Grissom Jr. was convicted in the 1990 murders of Joan Butler and two other women, although their bodies have never been recovered. Grissom is serving a life sentence in Lansing, Kansas.

WORKS CONSULTED

Dan Mitrione, *Suddenly Gone*, New York, St. Martin's Paperbacks, 1996.

11. Audrey

On September 16, 1986, Vicki Wegerle, a 28-year-old wife and mother, was strangled in her Wichita home by an intruder who drove away in her car. On February 28, 2005, Dennis Rader, the BTK Killer, was formally charged with ten counts of first-degree murder, including that of Vicki Wegerle, whom he had stalked for some time, and to whom he referred in his own writings as "Project Piano." Rader is serving a series of life sentences at the El Dorado Correctional Facility in Kansas.

WORKS CONSULTED

Robert Beattie, *Nightmare in Wichita: The Hunt for the BTK Strangler*, New York, New American Library, 2005.

Carlton Smith, *The BTK Murders*, New York, St. Martin's True Crime Paperbacks, 2006.

12. Vicky

Donna Lass, age 25, worked as a nurse at the Sahara Casino in Lake Tahoe, California. Her last entry in the nurses' logbook was at 1:50 A.M. on September 6, 1970, and although her car was found parked at her apartment complex, she was not seen after leaving the casino. The following day, an unknown male called her landlord and employer, stating Lass wouldn't be returning to work due to a family emergency. There has been no trace of her since. A postcard purportedly from the Zodiac Killer was received by the San Francisco Chronicle on March 22, 1971, implying that Lass was one of his numerous victims. The Zodiac Killer has never been identified.

WORKS CONSULTED

Kieran Crowley, *Sleep My Little Dead: The True Story of the Zodiac Killer*, New York, St. Martin's True Crime Library, 1997.

Michael D. Kelleher and David Van Nuys, *This Is the Zodiac Speaking: Into the Mind of a Serial Killer*, New York, Praeger, 2008.

13. Mirasol

On July 13, 1966, Richard Speck broke into a nurses' hostel on Chicago's south side and killed eight of the nine nurses who lived there. The ninth nurse, Corazon Amarao, escaped death by hiding under a bed. She ultimately provided a description that led to Speck's arrest and conviction. Richard Speck died of a heart attack in an Illinois prison in 1991.

WORKS CONSULTED

Dennis L. Breo, *The Crime of the Century*, New York, Bantam, 1993.

Jack Altman and Marvin Ziporyn, *Born to Raise Hell: The Untold Story of Richard Speck—The Man, The Crime, The Trial*, New York, Grove Press, 1967.

Afterword

Murder. The murderer's image in the eye of the murdered.
They love reading about it. Man's head found in a garden.
Her clothing consisted of. How she met her death. Recent
outrage. The weapon used. Murderer is still at large. Clues.
A shoelace. The body to be exhumed. Murder will out.

—James Joyce, *Ulysses* (1922)

Like many other people, I've always been an enthusiastic reader of
that genre of non-fiction known, not always accurately, as "true crime."
What draws me to these fascinating stories is not the promise of a violent crime, but the lure of peripheral details. I've always been more
interested in victims than criminals (though most criminals, of course,
are victims themselves, in one way or another), and in writing *Thirteen
Girls*, I decided to focus wholly on the contingent details of each case,
getting rid of all the fat and filler. Enough has been said, for now, about
the Son of Sam, Ted Bundy, The Boston Strangler, Richard Speck and
the others, but how many of us, except those involved or obsessed,
can name a single one of their victims? The murderers themselves
have been magnified by the long shadows they cast over our cultural
imagination, but their victims remain unknown and unmourned, except by those who knew them best, or who, like me, have the kind of
interest in their lives that is commonly deemed "unhealthy."

This book was born at the crossroads where murder meets contingency, a place that offers a different view from that of formulaic crime narratives, which are generally written to suit the way we've been conditioned, by media and culture, to receive them. We're used to reading about victims and perpetrators, clues and signs, arrests and penalties. "True crime" has a linear, progressive trajectory; it tells of information and events, police and courtrooms, healing and closure. In *Thirteen Girls*, I wanted to do something different. I wanted to tell a series of stories that would question the social and cultural positioning of "true crime," and to question the ways we assign meaning to events that preoccupy us, however temporarily.

Every murder has its little nooks and crannies, and these are the spaces *Thirteen Girls* explores. Think of the stories in this book as a series of repressed, parallel texts to those that customarily take precedent in mainstream "true crime" narratives. The stories in *Thirteen Girls*, whether personal, forensic, accidental or conditional, are the forgotten, peripheral tales occasionally glimpsed in the spaces left by the "true crime" narratives we're used to, which is not to say the stories in this book are not also true, in their way. Each of these girls is a real person, and so are most of the secondary characters (such as their parents and families). Others are composites. Names have been changed to protect the living.

Thirteen Girls, then, is not about violent crime so much its fallout and sequelae. It considers the afterlife of murder through the eyes of the people it has affected, to a lesser or greater degree. The book is intended as both a psychological portrait of crime and a consideration of the ways in which our cultural obsession with violence and a need for "closure" stacks up against the emotional power of personal testimony.

It's true that these stories look unflinchingly at the fallout from violence against young women, yet although the murders referred to in this book are cruel and disturbing, the events themselves are not described in detail, as they are in most "true crime."

I was surprised, then, that the book was rejected by over a dozen publishers, all of whom were put off by what more than one referred to as its "unrelenting darkness."

"These are too tough for me," one publisher wrote to my agent. "I couldn't bear to read them all." "These stories are just too stark and unforthcoming to be satisfying," wrote another. "You are left only with a sense of ugly contingency and meaninglessness in the Big American Empty, and it is just not enough."

Ugly contingency and meaninglessness are not enough, but they are what we have. Most people turn to books to give them something more than what they already have: A payoff. But in real life, there is no payoff, no closure. The truth about dead girls is this: In the end, they are all forgotten.

Mikita Brottman

April, 2012

MIKITA BROTTMAN is a cultural critic, author, and psychoanalyst. Known for her interest in various cultural pathologies, she has written influentially on horror films, critical theory, animals, reading, psychoanalysis, and the work of the American folklorist, Gershon Legman. Her articles and case studies have appeared in *The American Journal of Psychoanalysis, New Literary History, American Imago* and *The Psychoanalytic Review.* She is a professor in the Department of Humanistic Studies at the Maryland Institute College of Art in Baltimore.

mikitabrottman.com